Speaking of:
CHILD CARE
Everything you wanted to know

Published by
Sterling Publishers Private Limited

Speaking of:
CHILD CARE
Everything you wanted to know

DR. SURAJ GUPTE, M.D.

A Sterling Paperback

STERLING PAPERBACKS
An imprint of
Sterling Publishers (P) Ltd.
A-59 Okhla Industrial Area, Phase-II,
New Delhi-110020.
Tel: 6331238, 6331241
Fax: 91-11-6331241 E-mail: ghai@nde.vsnl.net.in
www.sterlingpublishers.com

Speaking of Child Care: Everything you wanted to know
© 1991, Dr. Suraj Gupte, M.D.
First Edition 1983
Second Revised and Enlarged Edition 1991
Reprint 1995
ISBN 81 207 1795 3
Reprint 2001, 2002, 2004

Published by Sterling Publishers Pvt. Ltd., New Delhi-110 020.
Printed at : Sai Early Learners (P) Ltd.
Cover design by Adage Communications

Dedicated to
my Mummy and Daddy who always
give my efforts the necessary
blessings. They have been
a tower of strength and
inspiration in bringing
out this book

FOREWORD

It was at a World Book Fair that I first came across Dr. Suraj Gupte's book, *Know Your Child,* (now retitled *Speaking of Child Care: Everything You Wanted to Know)* a few years ago. Needless to say, I was highly impressed by its rich contents, simple and straightforward narration and practical rather than philosophical orientation. Nevertheless, little did I realise then that some day I would be bestowed the honour of writing a "Foreword" to this wonderful book.

The overall impression the new revised, updated and enlarged edition of the *Speaking of Child Care* leaves on a critical reader's mind is that a child brought up with right nutrition and rest of the health care, love, freedom and discipline enters the adolescence and later adulthood with security and confidence, holding virtually all the trump cards for success in life.

Not that Dr. Gupte says that, in raising children, no problems are encountered. There are, in fact, many! The book tells the parents how to prevent them and how to tackle them eminently. You will find in it all sorts of much-sought-after information, from conception through breast-feeding, love bonds, schooling etc., to adolescence and its problems, behaviour difficulties, discipline, medical problems, adoption and the like.

I must say that the reputed pediatrician, researcher, innovator, educationist and author, Dr. Suraj Gupte's *Speaking of Child Care* is a work of exceptional merit. It is strongly recommended. I am confident it will help parents, especially in the Indian subcontinent, to assist children grow up happily, well-adjusted and optimistic about the world around.

Prof. Michael Gray, *FRCOG*
Former WHO Advisor
(S-E Asia)
New York *Maternal & Child Health*

PREFACE TO THE SECOND EDITION

At the very outset, here's thanking the readers and reviewers who accorded the *Know Your Child* (now retitled *Speaking of Child Care: Everything You Wanted to Know*) a warm reception over the years. Unfortunately the book remained out of print for quite some time for reasons beyond my control. My apologies are due for this lapse!

The new edition is thoroughly revised and updated with fresh additions. The original aim of its being a spotlight on the "total child" is maintained. Hopefully, all this will enhance the practical utility of the book and contribute to the eventual goal of providing better child care.

I wish to record my special gratitudes to Prof. Michael Gray, FRCOG, Former WHO Advisor (S.-E. Asia), Maternal & Child Health, for writing a "Foreword" to the second edition of the volume and so warmly recommending the book to parents and others interested in child care.

I also acknowledge contribution of my wife, Shamma-Bakshi Gupte, who enriched my writings in many ways, particularly through excellent counselling based on her first hand experience in bringing up our two sweet children—daughter Novy and son Manu.

Finally, I shall continue welcoming the "feedback" for further enhancing the value of the book.

Suraj Gupte, M.D.

PREFACE TO THE FIRST EDITION

It is indeed exciting to plan a family, to wait for the arrival of the "little one" and to watch him grow, spreading his mind and abilities. Imagine the thrill it gives you as you watch him opening out, throwing a smile or responding to you in his own small way.

And, yet, the fact remains that during his upbringing, more often than not, you find yourself in a mess on trivial matters. How you wish someone had guided you about the right way to handle him, how to feed him, what to do when he cries, how to get him protected against certain illnesses and accidents, so on and so forth. What is happening in a child's mind and what upsets him emotionally do concern you. But, what a pity that you find yourself helpless and not able to do a thing that will eventually benefit the child.

This book aims at providing the answers. It explains all that is necessary to know for young parents in India and other developing countries about child-rearing—right from "how it starts" to the "stormy teens" including recognition of various medical problems.

Is this book meant only for parents? No, it is for everybody having something to do with the "growing child". Nurses, midwives, school teachers, students of home-science and housecraft and general practitioners whose practice involves care of the children in particular will find it very rewarding.

So, here's wishing you happy and rewarding reading to help your children grow up happily and well.

Suraj Gupte, M.D.

CONTENTS

PREGNANCY BY CHOICE: THE FACTS ABOUT CONTRACEPTION

1. Shortly after the brief honeymoon in Simla, the love birds, Anu, 18, and Gaurav Chaudhuri, 22, were no longer ecstatic.

   For, following a visit to the lady doctor for Anu's early morning sickness coupled with nausea, vomiting and loss of appetite, she had turned out to be, as Dr. Sushma Bhardwaj put it, "in the family way". Pregnant at just 18 and yet to complete her degree in arts! And, hell, her hubby was no better: he had barely made a beginning in his career. Were they really ready for responsible parenthood? "Of course, not," they answered almost simultaneously.

2. Our next-door neighbour, Mrs. Raina, while busy bringing up a cute 6-months-old daughter, has conceived again. To quote her husband, Mr. Vipin Raina: "The very thought of another child all too soon gives me creeps." Adds Mrs. Raina: "With our meagre income, I wonder how we shall be able to do justice to two children.... And, imagine the increasing stress and strain on my own body."

3. Singhs, a happy-go-lucky couple, are rather gloomy because, though they were keen to postpone the arrival of a child for a couple of years, Meena Singh has become pregnant. "Our economic condition and the stress of the jobs do not permit us this luxury at present," they say.

4. The other day, I ran into this young couple, Pathaks. What surprised me was that, despite four children surrounding them, the wife was in fairly an advanced stage of pregnancy. To my indirect query, the husband replied: "Well, well, this is all God's will." Nevertheless, they were unhappy that they would have to cope with so many children.

The hundred million dollar question is: Who's responsible for the unhappiness of Chaudhuris, Rainas, Singhs and Pathaks? You'll agree with me that none else but the couples themselves. They should have used one or the other of the birth control measures, the subject matter of this chapter.

So, here we go, talking about the salient details of various contraceptive means.

Natural means

If you and your husband practise contraception without using any equipment, you are adopting natural means. Two categories of natural methods are employed. In the first category are included abstinence or celibacy, coitus interruptus, safe period, and breast-feeding. In the second category, you—yes, I mean the wife—employs self-recognition of certain signs as an aid to determine ovulation, the time when there is peak chance to conceive.

Abstinence or celibacy means complete sexual abstinence unless and until the couple has decided to have the baby. This involves suppression of natural "force". This may well be practicable with some people but is surely no reasonable method of contraception to be advocated to the couples at large.

The noted authority, Kinsley, mentions categorically how forced abstinence led to nervous breakdown in one or the other spouse in his famous study on the sex habits of the Europeans under the spell of a particular quack sexologist.

Coitus interruptus consists in the husband's withdrawing the organ as soon as he reaches the orgasm. He ejaculates the semen outside the vagina rather than into it.

This method, as you can see, is very simple. It costs nothing. And, no appliance is needed. This is a traditional method and continues to be quite popular to date.

But, you may well ask: Is it foolproof? Does it indeed give the couple full satisfaction?

Taking up the first query—well, it is not a foolproof means at all. A slight mistake in timing the withdrawal of the male organ may lead to deposition of some semen into the vagina. Mind you, all that is needed to cause conception is a drop of it, perhaps less to tell you the truth.

As regards the second point—well, the method certainly does not give the couple full satisfaction. More often than not, it has been found as the cause of emotional upset and anxiety.

Safe period or rhythm method consists in having coitus during a period when least or no chance of conception exists.

In a woman with 28-days regular cycle, seven days before the forthcoming menstrual period are considered the safest. Generally speaking, 3 to 5 days of active bleeding, 3 to 4 days after the period and some 7 to 10 days preceding the period are more or less safe. Some 8 to 10 days between the two periods are vulnerable for conception. The doctors call them "unsafe period".

An oft-asked question is: Doctor, if intercourse is done during the safe period only, can one let one's hair down and relax? Well, the answer is *NO* with capital letters.

Why? Experience has shown that the safe period method fails 1 in 5 instances. The failure is usually ascribed to mistaken calculations, taking chances or lack of cooperation between the husband and the wife.

Remember, good lady, this method is never, never to be recommended to women with irregular menstrual cycles. Understand?

Breast-feeding is said to offer some safeguard against an unwanted pregnancy. To be of value in this context, it should be exclusive rather than be supplemented by the other milk or soft foods.

Nevertheless, I don't think in individual cases, one can bank upon breast-feeding as a dependable way of birth control. All the same, the fact remains that breast-feeding is the best feeding.

Basal body temperature method consists in maintaining very carefully daily body temperature record. You are supposed to record the temperature just before getting out of bed in the morning, not anytime during the day. An elevation by 0.3 to 0.5°C is a sign of ovulation. The elevation in boby temperature is maintained until the onset of next period.

If coitus is restricted to post-ovulatory period which starts 3 days after the temperature elevation and continues up to the beginning of menstruation, this method becomes quite dependable.

Its snag is that celibacy is warranted for almost half of the menstrual cycle, before the ovulation as well.

Ovulation method, also called Billings' method or cervical mucus method, consists in observing regularly by the woman her cervical mucus discharge. The mucus, if watery, clear, resembling a raw egg white, smooth, slippery and profuse, points to ovulation. No sooner does ovulation stop than it becomes thick and scanty.

As you can appreciate, these few days of ovulation would require abstinence on your and your husband's part.

Symptothermic method consists in daily palpation of the opening of the womb into the vagina. If the opening gradually becomes patent and the cervix soft, in all probability, ovulation is round the corner.

If the cervical secretion in the vagina shows an increase and also becomes watery, smooth and slippery like the white of an egg, chances are that the time of ovulation is approaching. Once ovulation is over, secretion lessens and becomes thick.

This method combines palpation and cervical mucus methods and, therefore, double-checks the interpretations.

Chemical means

Douching consists in washing the vagina with a weak solution of soap and water, a solution of vinegar, lemon, tepid water or some antiseptic solution. It is claimed that this method leads to creation of an environment in the vagina that proves fatal to the male eggs, *sperms.*

Though douching is frequently employed as a domestic means for safeguarding against pregnancy, particularly in the rural settings, its value is, at its best, dubious.

Contraceptive foam tablets, jellies, pastes, creams etc., introduced deep into vagina, constitute a very popular birth control measure. These agents are supposed to block the entry of the sperms into the uterus, slow down their speed and kill or render invalid a proportion of them.

Employed as such, the success rate in terms of prevention of pregnancy by these agents is around 75 per cent. However, success rate zooms very high when they are used in combination with the condom.

Mind you, though foam tablets are cheap, jellies, pastes and creams are really very expensive.

Mechanical means

This group refers to devices which aim at interrupting the meeting of the husband's sperm with the wife's ovum.

Condom, also called rubber, leather or sheath, is a device for use by the husband. It is rolled over the penis, when erect, so as to cover it fully. During coitus, semen collects within its teat rather than in the vagina. Once the act is over, the condom is discarded. Each piece is meant to be used once only.

The market is flooded with various proprietary brands of condom. Always go for a good quality stuff. Else, you may have to cut a sorry figure.

The most popular Indian condom, *Nirodh*, is highly subsidised by the Government of India. If obtained from a Family Welfare Centre, it costs nothing. Even in the market, all that you need to pay is 25 paise for a pack of three pieces. What is remarkable is that it is made of a high quality stuff.

If it is used in conjunction with a spermicidal chemical, failure rate is virtually negligible. Another plus point is that it also protects against sexually-transmitted diseases.

Of course, there are some minus points about condom. As for example, some couples grumble that since the genitals of the partners are slightly interrupted by the sheath, it takes away some pleasure. Also, there is some chance of the condom tearing off or slipping off during coitus. This, to tell you the truth, appears to be related to carelessness in employing it rather than the inherent defect in the device.

Diaphragm, a mechanical barrier, is made of synthetic rubber or plastic. It is 5 to 10 cm. in diameter and is meant to be inserted well up and high into the vagina before coitus. What is not to be forgotten is that it must remain for at least six hours after the act in this very position.

You are supposed to consult your doctor for the right size of the diaphragm for you. Also, make a solid note that it is of added gain to smear it with a contraceptive cream or jelly before insertion into the vagina.

The merit of diaphragm lies in its being relatively cheap. If you exercise proper care in handling it, it lasts for quite a long time without losing its effectiveness. Unlike condom, it does not interfere with sexual satisfaction.

But, then, the snag is that you have got to consult a doctor or a midwife to fit it in the beginning.

Intra-uterine contraceptive devices (IUCD) are innumerable but the one most popular and officially recommended by the Family Welfare Department of Government of India is what is called *Lippe's loop*. It has stood the test of time in most of the countries.

Lippe's loop consists of a loop, inserter, plunger, guard and threads. The threads made of nylon keep projecting into the vagina as a reminder that the device is still in place.

The device should best be introduced at the end of the menstrual period by a qualified doctor in a hospital or a clinic.

In India, IUCD facility is available fairly widely in a network of centres throughout urban and rural areas.

A woman who has gone in for IUCD must:

a. See the doctor regularly after the first menstrual period to make sure that the loop is in place;
b. Check regularly the thread of the loop. In case she fails to find it, look up the doctor;
c. Visit the doctor as and when she finds persistent vaginal bleeding, low backache, pain in the tummy, pain in the thighs, vaginal discharge, expulsion of the loop, persistent fever not explainable by any obvious cause and doubtful conception;
d. Have regular checkup from the doctor, initially every 3 months, then after every 6 months followed by once a year.

There are advantages in wearing a loop. It is inexpensive and simple to insert—in a matter of minutes. It may be retained for several years, if desired, and yet it is an absolutely reversible contraceptive method.

The success rate is as high as 95 to 98 per cent. Whatever risk of pregnancy exists is in the first year of use. In subsequent years, risk is negligible.

More recently, our Family Welfare Department has introduced in the National Family Welfare Programme the *copper IUCD* which is supposed to have some advantages over the Lippe's loop, namely:

a. Less loss of blood during the period;
b. Less chance of spontaneous expulsion;
c. Better tolerance by young women who are yet to bear a child;
d. May act as a valuable post-coital contraceptive, provided that it is inserted within 3 to 5 days of unprotected sexual union.

Oral contraceptive pill

The contraceptive pill is a hormonal preparation that suppresses the release of egg, i.e., the ovulation, in the woman.

The so-called *combined pill*, containing small amounts of two hormones (oestrogen and progestrogen) is the most effective reversible method of contraception available at present.

Taken regularly, the combined pill (also called *21 days pill*) offers almost 100 per cent protection. It is required to be taken orally by the woman for 21 days, starting on the fifth day of the menstrual cycle, followed by a break of 7 days during which time menstruation occurs.

The second type of pill is what is designated as *micro pill*. Also called *28-day pill*, it contains only one hormone, i.e., progestrogen and is required to be administered everyday of the month without breaking the sequence. It is said to be less effective than the combined pill.

Remember that some users of oral pill may have such side-effects as breakthrough bleeding, suppression of lactation if pill is started soon after previous childbirth, excessive weight gain and psychological depression.

If you are considering to take the pill, do remember to see your doctor and have his advice. Generally speaking, the pill should be used by women who are yet to cross the age of 35 years. The doctor would see to it that you do not suffer from migraine, epilepsy, diabetes, severe allergy, asthma, eczema and such other diseases that contradict its use.

Once you are on the pill, after obtaining the doctor's advice, do make it a point to get your medical examination at least once a year.

Let me tell you frankly that today more and more women are taking to the oral pill. This is, perhaps, the only method of contraception that does not operate directly at the time of the sexual act, thus having a lot to say in its favour, particularly from the point of psychological and emotional needs of the couple.

The new low dose pill, *Mala-D*, specially made for the Indian women, is available at a highly subsidized price of Rs. 2 per cycle.

Injectable contraceptives

Two forms of injectable hormonal contraceptives, administered intramuscularly, are now available: first, depot-medroxyprogesterone acetate (DMPA); second, norethisterone enantate (NET-EN).

They act primarily by suppressing ovulation.

The injection is required to be given every 90 days in case of DMPA and every 60 days in case of NET-EN.

This measure gives protection from pregnancy in 99 per cent women.

Moreover, it is a safe, effective and reliable means requiring mimimal or no motivation.

Nevertheless, some users may suffer from disturbance of the normal menstrual cycle.

2

WONDERS OF WAITING FOR THE BABY

How it all begins

Now that a couple have decided to go ahead and have a baby, let us see how it all happens—I mean how a new human being starts its roots within the mother.

What is conception? To understand the phenomenon, you need to have some idea of the process of *ovulation*. In simple words, it means shedding of ripe eggs (ova) from the ovary, the female egg-producing organ. The ovum enters a tube that joins the uterus. One of the would-be-father's innumerable sperms (again the sort of male eggs), provided available, may meet it and bury itself in the woman's own ripe egg. The thus-produced sperm-and-ovum combination shortly divides into equal new cells.

What is quite fascinating is that each of the two new cells has a fundamental structure of the original combined cell. In simple words, it contains half of the chromosomes (bodies carrying inherited characters from parents to child) from the father and half of these from the mother. It is, therefore, at this very early stage that the child's inheritance is decided.

The cluster of cells resulting from the sperm-and-ovum meeting in a few days passes from the tube down into the uterus. In the uterus a thick warm lining has been anxiously awaiting the arrival of a fertilised ovum. It is here that the cluster buries itself firmly for further growth. Thus fertilisation and implantation together constitute what has been called *conception*. It marks the cessation of *menstruation*. If, on the other hand, the thick warm lining fails to receive a fertilised ovum, it gets shed in the form of menstrual flow—a processa which is repeated as menstrual period very month in every normal woman until she reaches menopause.

Recognising pregnancy

Most experienced mothers seldom find much difficulty in recognising is pregnancy. This may not be true in the case of young mothers who are jumping into such an encounter for the first time. Even they find senior women in the house quite prompt in identifying the occurrence of pregnancy and apprising them of it.

Stopping of the menstrual period is usually the earliest sign of pregnancy. It should, however, be remembered that a highly strung woman may miss her period just out of anxiety rather than as a result of conception. Secondly, the menstrual period may be missed in other women with irregular and scanty periods. In any case, as and when a suspicion about occurrence of pregnancy arises it is advisable to consult your doctor who knows how to confirm it.

Morning sickness usually accompanies early stages of pregnancy. The woman wakes up with nausea and may vomit. In subsequent weeks it slowly subsides.

By the end of the first month changes occurring in the breasts, in preparation for producing milk for the baby, cause their fullness and tenderness.

By the third month a pregnant woman becomes aware of a mass in the lower abdomen which now starts protruding.

The so-called "quickening" refers to the movements of the foetus (baby in the womb) felt on palpation of the abdomen of the mother. The sign occurs as the pregnancy advances.

As soon as it becomes clear that pregnancy has resulted, arrangements should be made to attend an *Antenatal Clinic* at a hospital, health centre or dispensary. It is advisable to have good medical care right at the outset rather than when pregnancy is fairly advanced.

How long will the pregnancy last?

A well-founded query in the mind of every pregnant mother, particularly if this is going to be her first-born!

As a convention it is held that an average pregnancy lasts 280 days (40 weeks) from the first day of the last menstrual period the woman had. Since it is very diffcult to be sure of the actual date of conception, the conventional method comes in handy as a convenient way to calculate the expected date of delivery (EDD).

For an approximate EDD, add 7 days to the first day of last period and go 3 months behind or 9 months ahead.

Three trimesters of pregnancy

The first three months are the most crucial inasmuch as that baby's organs such as heart, brain, kidneys, eyes etc., are formed during this trimester of pregnancy. Infections, such as German measles, during this period can do grave harm to the foetus.

How the baby grows inside the womb

The small bundle of cells implanted in the wall of the womb are differentiated in the first three weeks into two major groups. The first group forms in due course, arms and legs, and heart and lungs. The second group forms part of the umblical cord that joins the foetus to the placenta, propularly known as *after-births*. The latter is a saucer-shaped mass of blood vessels and soft tissue. It is through this that the *foetus* obtains its nutrition from the mother. It also provides certain hormones for the maintenance of the pregnancy.

As the foetus approaches fourth week, a head, a trunk and arm-and leg-buds have already developed. It is encased in a waterproof membrane. The water in the case keeps the baby protected from outside shock and also keeps it warm.

The sixth week shows development of remarkable features. The embryo measures about an inch in length and weighs 1/30th of an ounce. It has taken the shape of a human face with eyes, nose, ears, lips and tongue and buds of milk teeth buried in the minute gums. Muscles, skin and a soft skeleton as also a tiny brain and heart with minute blood vessels are there. The stomach has begun to produce the digestive juices, so are the liver and kidneys making a beginning on their future task.

At the end of the eighth week, external sex organs show up. However, it is nearly impossible to make out the baby's sex from the appearance of these ambiguous organs.

Between 16 and 24 weeks the baby's heartbeat can be heard by a doctor.

By the end of 24th week, the foetus is around 12 inches in length. Its weight is about 1.5 pounds. In a healthy woman, it should increase its weight nearly five times in the last trimester of pregnancy. It is during this period that the mother may become increasingly conscious of the baby "kicking" inside the womb. Many authorities believe that the greater the kicking and thumping—to the extent of exhausting the mother—the higher the chances of the baby to grow into an active adult who will always be on the move. Professor W.E. Clark has in his anthology, *On Infancy to Adulthood*, quoted Freud as saying, "a baby who lies quietly in mother's tummy is a candidate for becoming an easygoing individual."

It is during these last 12 weeks that the baby attempts sucking his fingers and some of the such other skills that he is likely to need after birth. He may attempt to cry as well, without producing a sound.

Antenatal check-up and booking

As soon as a woman becomes aware of the pregnancy (or even suspects it), she should have an antenatal check-up and then follow it regularly throughout the pregnancy. A woman who fails to take care of herself during pregnancy is less likely to give birth to a healthy baby.

At the first antenatal check-up, the doctor would like to have the pregnant woman's medical history, make a physical examination and do a few tests. Do not fuss when he asks questions about the present and past state of your health, as also about your earlier pregnancies (if any), the family history, your diet and the like. Sitting over some information that may have a bearing on the course or outcome of pregnancy may well prove dangerous. Mind you, your doctor is not superhuman. He needs your cooperation to anticipate and to help you. Do not leave everything to his imagination.

A thorough physical examination includes examination of the birth passage (the so-called *pre-vaginal examination*) and checking the blood pressure (BP). It is also important to make a record of the weight and height. The doctor may also like to have certain measurements of the pelvis, the bony cage through which the baby will ultimately pass during delivery.

The laboratory tests which the doctor would like to carry out include (i) blood examination for level of haemoglobin to ascertain if anaemia is present and for blood grouping (particularly if Rh positive or negative), (ii) urine examination for pus cells and albumin (a protein), and (iii) stool examination for eggs for intestinal parasites such as roundworm, hookworm, giardia and amoeba.

You should attend the antenatal clinic (or perhaps your obstetrician can do it at your own place) once a month until the seventh month. After the seventh month such a check-up should be once in a fortnight. During the ninth month, it should be every week until delivery.

At the time of antenatal check-ups, the would-be-mother should discuss with the doctor any emotional problems or apprehensions (about the pregnancy) she may have, which may be causing undue tension. Remember, it is not just your physical health that is important. You should be healthy emotionally too.

Most pregnancies with good antenatal care would end up happily. Yet the pregnant woman should remain vigilant and alert. Report to your doctor if the morning sickness is severe and adamantly persistent, any vaginal bleeding, swelling over feet and ankles, blurring of vision, persistent headache/giddiness, leakage of water from womb or cessation of foetal movements.

Care of the mother-to-be

Diet

The pregnant woman needs a well-balanced adult diet. It will be advisable to include fresh vegetables, fruits, milk, cheese, eggs, meat and fish in the daily food.

There is no truth in the saying that the pregnant woman should eat enough for two. Too much of eating may cause extra weight gain, putting excessive load on the already overburdened liver and kidneys. Excess weight is also likely to increase her discomfort when the abdomen becomes enlarged. There is also risk of permanent marking on her skin and impairment of her figure after childbirth.

That a pregnant woman should eat very little to safeguard against difficult delivery is again a myth. Get it out of your system.

What, then, is the precise recommendation? Well, you should eat a well-balanced diet and little extra of everything that you normally take when you are pregnant. This will amount to some 300 additional calories everyday.

A well-balanced diet does not mean expensive foods but foods that provide energy, body-building stuff and protective stuff. Energy-giving foods include rice, wheat, maize, potatoes, sugar, jaggery, fats and oils. Body-building foods (high protein stuffs) include pulses, peas, beans, nuts, milk, meat, fish and eggs. Protective foods include fruits (orange, banana, mango) and vegetables (carrot, spinach, methi, mustard leaves, mint) which are rich in vitamins and minerals.

Alcohol and smoking should decidedly be given up by the pregnant woman. There is now convincing evidence that smoking, especially in the last trimester, may cause growth retardation of the baby that is in the womb. Not only that, his brain may also be affected.

Coffee and tea in moderation are permissible.

Clothing

Ordinary dress will do for the first four months. After the fifth month, the pregnant woman should make it a point to wear loose clothing. The garment should not constrict the waist. Instead it should hang from the shoulders, hardly putting any pressure on the abdomen. You may get tailored or readymade maternity dresses—attractive, loose and comfortable. These should have fairly good allowance for further expansion.

It is necessary to wear a well-fitting brassiere to prevent excessive stretching of the skin under the weight of the large breasts.

Exercise and rest

The pregnant woman needs at least eight hours sleep during night. An afternoon nap is desirable. Every now and then, during daily routine work, she should sit down for a few minutes and relax.

An evening walk done in moderation does a lot of good. Mind you, diminish it slowly as the pregnancy advances. As the delivery date is round the corner, short strolls within or around the house are good enough.

Exercise, in one or the other form, is strongly recommended. Any exercise or a sport in which risks of falls or blows are considerable is best avoided. The same can be said about long and tiresome journeys.

All said and done, remember that "fatigue is the enemy of the pregnant woman."

Emotional health

The time-honoured advice that "pregnant woman should think of beautiful things to ensure a happy baby" continues to hold good even today. A mother who learns to relax and enjoy her pregnancy (never mind even if you have to talk over your worries and problems to experts or other family members to come to terms with your anxiety state) will come to the labour room with a relaxed body and a calm, peaceful mind. She is most likely going to have relatively easier labour. Such a labour leaves the mother happy, cheerful and relaxed. She, in turn, transmits her feelings to her baby, making him relaxed and contended and easy to establish on a happy feeding schedule. That is exactly what you need!

Physical health

Well-nourished mothers who are also free from diseases are known to bear strains of pregnancy better. They give birth to newborns with greater birth weight and higher vitality for growth and development.

It is a sound policy to avoid getting in contact with German measles (rubella) during early months of pregnancy. Else, the baby may be born with variable physical defects.

Drugs

Certain medicines may have adverse effects on the foetus. You should, therefore, avoid taking any drug—yes, this includes even the indigenous herbal medicaments—without doctor's advice, especially in the early half of pregnancy. Your doctor may, however, prescribe for you iron, calcium or vitamin pills in case you are anaemic and/or nutritionally lacking in vitamins and calcium. What is important is that you should leave medication to him, even such commonly-used ones as tranquillizers, paracetamol or aspirin.

Avoid smoking and drinking like the plague.

Preparing for the breast-feeding

Every pregnant mother must appreciate that the ideal and the most natural method of feeding the baby, at least during the first few months, is breast-feeding. It protects the baby from quite a few infections and diseases and assists in establishing a healthy mother-child relationship. The figure-conscious woman would find an additional gain from breast-feeding. It helps her to shed the much-too-much fat collected during pregnancy and contributes a great deal towards their attempt to slim down.

Proper care of breasts, in preparation for feeding the forthcoming baby, should, therefore, begin during pregnancy *per se*. A well-fitting brassiere and a protective pad are helpful. It should also be seen that the nipples are kept clean and made softer and longer by massage etc.

Shopping for the forthcoming baby

Now that the baby is expected in another month or so, the mother should get ready with his material requirements. These are:

1. Baby cot with sides to protect against rolling over. No pillow is needed but a foam rubber mattress will be ideal. Sheets for mattresses as also plastic or rubber sheets to protect mattresses from soiling are needed.

2. Baby bathtub (plastic).

3. Nappies or diapers, made of gauze or cotton towel material, together with a pad of cotton for wiping the soiled buttocks of the baby, some safety pins and nappy bucket.

4. Clothing: Napkins, vests, shirts without buttons or zips, head caps, sweaters, socks, blankets etc.

5. Feeding Equipment: What is strongly and without reservations recommended is that mother must breast-feed the infant unless there is a solid case for giving artificial feeding. In the latter case, she should be equipped with properly-designed feeding bottles and nipples, brushes to clean these, milk powder and a container if cow's milk is not regularly available and a kettle for sterilising the bottles.

6. *Pram* will prove handy for carrying the baby once he is beyond 3 to 4 months of age.

7. Baby soap, powder, cream and oil.

3
HUSBAND'S ROLE DURING WIFE'S CONFINEMENT

The other day, I ran into an old, old friend, Dinesh Prabhakar.

"So, man, Neera is in the family way, I am told. Going to be the proud father? By the way, when should we expect the big news? Before long, I guess," I virtually bombarded the old boy.

Imagine his reaction!

"Yes, of course, Neera is expecting. But, then, what is so great about it?" he replied. "On the contrary, I am scared like hell. Right away I am beginning to be in hot soup. The actual arrival of the baby is bound to cause worse problems—like upsetting our routine, our way of life, and, what is worrying me most, adversely affecting my career which is yet to take off the way I indeed want."

"Strange. But, weren't you and Neera longing for a baby so passionately until recently?" I questioned him.

His answer: "Well—yes, we are. But, now that it is going to happen in actuality, I am at my wit's end. Confused! Utterly confused!"

Are you too sailing in the same boat, my friend—apprehensive that the arrival of the baby would shatter your lifestyle?

In the first place, remember that one of the several things you had promised your partner during courtship and/or at the time of wedding was: "I shall take care of you." Now that she is expecting the baby, it is time to help her, keep her morale high and cheer her up. It will cost nothing but do her a lot of good.

A good husband is a good friend, counsellor, playmate and what not. Learn all that you can about your wife's pregnancy as also childbirth along with her. Watching the things happen under your nose will make it most interesting for both of you.

Try to read the books or brochures that she reads. Discuss the things with her. But, for God's sake, do not frighten her. A young man would borrow dreadful stories from his friends about childbirth and whisper these straight into his wife's ears. Before long, she would develop such nasty ideas about pregnancy and childbirth that she would virtually want to run away from the idea of having the baby. That is the worst role a husband play.

Also, ensure that bad literature does not reach her. Such stuff may be interesting to read but leaves very adverse effects on the mind of pregnant women.

Accompany your wife to the doctor, in the hospital or clinic, for antenatal check-up or for reservation of room to organise her future hospitalisation for delivery. Once she finds herself convinced that you have made nice arrangements for her delivery, she will feel quite confident that all is going to be fine.

Don't forget that it is not only your wife's problem to follow the doctor's advice but yours too. Listen to the doctor carefully. Don't lose your temper if she makes slips. Make her understand. Let her see reason. And, do all this with a smile rather than with a rod.

No doubt, you're a busy person. Yet, you are supposed to find time—enough of it indeed—to spend with her, to listen to her problems and to her fears with patience, to make sound deductions and then sort out the things to her satisfaction. More often than not, the issues are simply "minor". All that is needed is to reassure the wife.

Never, never, give her an anxious look. The more worry she sees on your face, the more unhappy she will become. Don't get jittery if she gets tired easily, shows her irritation frequently, and is time and again going into depression or temper tantrums. Her behaviour may be quite strange. One moment she wants to be left alone and the next she grumbles a lot at your "indifference" to her in leaving her alone. All this, mind you, is normal in pregnancy. Even if you feel upset, don't let your mental tension show. Little wonder, it is hard and disturbing to find her "feeling sick" time and again. But if you, at this stage, begin to lose your head, then you will make things harder still.

Also, don't make the mistake of surrounding her with all the family members, displaying undue concern as and when she is not well. You'll only be making her more nervous. For, she is bound to think she is "very, very sick".

When the time for delivery comes, try to be at her side. If she wants you to be present at the time of "actual" labour, don't hesitate to do so, provided the doctor permits. The modern opinion is that the husband's role is to provide the wife with strength of his presence at childbirth. It seems, as borne out by the psychologists, a crucial factor in making childbirth a positive event. In other words, the woman's perceptions of the world are usually far healthier when her husband is present by her side.

Finally, this is what the noted psychiatrist, Joost Meerlo has to say: "The psychological impact of the father on the emotional development of the child has long been overlooked .... The example set by the father is vital for shaping the destiny and eventual emotional independence of the adult-to-be.... The joint relationship of parents with the child begins at birth. As a matter of fact, if the husband is absent at the supreme moment when the woman gives birth, it may have an adverse effect on her. Later on, it may not be easy for the husband to reclaim his place, now unsurped during his wife's labour by substitute figures (obstetrician, family doctor, anaesthetist)."

Let me conclude, my friend, that if you care to share your wife's pregnancy with her and are as well informed as she is on what is involved, you will be able to give her the much-needed assurance and support.

For, undoubtedly, there is no other way to look forward to the arrival of the little stranger with love and longing! Right?

4

SOME COMMON DISORDERS IN PREGNANCY

Pregnancy is a unique experience for the mother. While the "new life" is growing inside her womb, she is given to dreaming beautiful dreams. That's all very fine. "In fact, it is very much desirable," if I may quote a world-renowned obstetrician.

Like any normal individual with responsibilities which are special and additional, putting extra load on her systems, a pregnant woman may, however, suffer from certain medical problems. The special significance of these problems is inasmuch as that these may have adverse effect on progress and outcome of pregnancy.

Anaemia

Believe it or not, on an average, total blood volume during pregnancy shoots up by about 45 per cent. As a result of high dilution of the body blood, ordinary technique of blood examination will show anaemia (apparent) with haemoglobin level between 10 and 11g per cent.

True, during pregnancy a woman saves about 25 mg of iron since she is no more losing blood in menstrual periods. But then the foetus needs about 400 mg of iron, the placenta 150 mg and lactation 300 mg for the pregnancy and the first three months of lactation. Thus, the requirement of a pregnant woman is much higher than what she saves. Now it is easy to understand why most pregnant women suffer from iron-deficiency anaemia if an extra amount of iron is not administered to them. Such other problems as can accompany pregnancy (poor dietary intake, worm infestations, chronic infections like tuberculosis) usually further aggravate existing anaemia. These factors may cause vitamin B_{12} and folic acid deficiency in addition, thereby introducing an element of megaloblastic anaemia.

Anaemia in pregnancy causes vague but widespread manifestations. The woman develops pallor of skin, nails and conjunctiva underlying the lids. There is loss of appetite, giddiness and insomnia (sleeplessness). She gets tired easily and has a feeling of being unwell. She may become increasingly conscious of heartbeat (palpitations) which becomes quite fast (tachycardia). Nails may become brittle and flattened (platynechia) or frankly spoon-shaped with a definite concavity (koilonychia).

In advanced cases, she may begin to become breathless on little exertion. Swelling over feet and ankles occurs in some anaemic women.

Raw, red and swollen tongue, indigestion and difficulty in swallowing (dysphagia) are seen in many a case.

Remember, anaemia can have an adverse effect not only on the mother but on the baby as well. If you are going to neglect it, your baby runs the risk of being a low-birth-weight infant. And that is not a small risk.

If you are pregnant and anaemic as well, chances are you have not been taking your doctor's advice seriously. Or, maybe you have not as yet had regular antenatal check-up. Report to your doctor immediately. He will get your blood and stools (maybe some other things also) tested.

You must cooperate with your doctor in treating your anaemia. He would expect you to take a diet that is rich in iron. But, you also need medicinal iron which he may like to give you as tablets or injection(s). If your anaemia is quite significant and pregnancy is fairly advanced, the doctor may want to raise your haemoglobin through blood transfusion.

Severe and obstinate vomiting

In some nervous and hypersensitive pregnant women, what begins as *morning sickness* becomes severe and persists, occurring several times a day. The vomitus may contain blood. All too soon, the woman stops accepting food and a little later even water is rejected. She becomes anorexic and constipated. Excessive thirst, dryness of the mouth and fall in the amount of urine results. The blood pressure falls and the pulse becomes fast and weak. She presents a picture of wasting and misery.

Treatment of this problem, *hyperemesis gravidarum*, should be left to the doctor and his team. Hospitalisation is essential.

What the pregnant woman must do to safeguard against the above-mentioned serious condition is to take adequate care of the so-called morning sickness which may be a predecessor to hyperemesis gravidarum.

A cup of weak tea or a fruit drink together with sweet biscuits should be taken in a recumbent position. She should sit up only after this drink and eat on waking up in the morning. During the day, she should take small amounts of carbohydrate-rich foods at frequent intervals, and avoid fats, fish, meat and soups.

Toxaemias of pregnancy

Pre-eclampsia is by far the commonest manifestation of toxaemias of pregnancy. Its earliest signs are high blood pressure and puffiness of the eyes, gain in weight and swelling over ankles and feet. Generally, swelling of the ankles are found spreading up the leg. Swelling, called oedema, may spread to other parts of the body. In severe cases, even external genitals may become swollen. Examination of urine will show presence of albumin, a protein.

Such a woman may complain of malaise, lassitude, headache, visual disturbances, vomiting and abdominal pain.

Pregnant women who are regularly attending an antenatal clinic should find little difficutly in having pre-eclampsia diagnosed at an early stage. It usually occurs in the second half of pregnancy period.

As a part of its management, your doctor will advise you to have complete bed rest and to reduce your salt intake. He will also prescribe a sedative, a diuretic and an hypotensive drug to get rid of the "water logging" and to bring down the blood pressure.

If you are overweight at the outset of pregnancy, you must reduce it. Also, do not let anaemia develop and see that your blood pressure is within normal range. All this will help you to keep pre-eclampsia at an arm's length.

Eclampsia includes all the manifestations of pre-eclampsia but in addition there are convulsions and coma also. It may occur during pregnancy, labour or after childbirth.

The disease is very, very serious and may prove fatal.

Hospitalisation is a must for adequate management. Most good hospitals have special Eclampsia rooms which have maximum quietness.

Chances of foetal death in eclamptic mothers are 25 per cent higher than in normal women. Also foetal growth retardation is a common observation.

The singlemost important contributory factor to the well being of the newborn in this condition is a good antenatal care. In its absence the progress of the disease remains unchecked, leading to a fatal outcome.

Diabetes mellitus

In half or even more of the pregnant women with diabetes the disease is known to be present before pregnancy occurs. The woman must apprise her doctor with this information rather than to leave it to him to detect it during antenatal check-up. Even if she is not aware of it, she should report to him such manifestations as increased thirst, greater frequency of micturition, increased appetite or itching in the region of the vulva. Remember, diabetics are more prone to develop toxaemias of pregnancy.

Management of pregnancy complicated with diabetes is best done by an obstetrician in collaboration with a physician.

Foetus of such a woman runs the risk of dying anytime during pregnancy. This risk is greater during the last month. The baby is likely to be larger and heavier than an average baby born at full term.

Be mentally prepared if you are such a mother. The chances are that either you would have to undergo a caesarean section or surgical induction of labour. The large, oedematous baby should immediately be examined by a child specialist. He requires special care. Despite his being overweight, he needs to be treated as *premature* if delivered before term.

Malaria

Return of malaria in the Indian subcontinent poses a big challenge. High swinging fever as a result of malaria, complicating pregnancy, abortion, premature labour and foetal death, may occur. Deterioration in the mother's health is a rule. In malaria, especially when it has caused severe anaemia also, difficulties in childbirth complicate the picture. Anaemia and poor material resistance predisposes to superadded infections.

If your pregnancy has somehow been complicated by malaria, do cooperate with your doctor in curing malaria. Remember pregnancy is not a contra-indication for using antimalaria drugs. Do not be taken in by the loose talks that antimalarial agents cause abortion. Risk, if any, is just very slight. At any rate, it is practically zero compared to the dangers involved in not treating the infection. The mother's death may even occur, if malaria is left untreated.

Disorders of urinary tract

Cystitis is a bacterial infection of the urinary bladder. Painful micturition (dysuria), episodes of retention of urine and fever should arouse suspicion about its presence.

Your doctor will get the diagnosis confirmed by the presence of red blood cells, pus cells and bacteria (the last-named are grown in culture discs).

He will prescribe chemotherapeutic drug(s) to get rid of the infection. Don't forget to take plenty of fluids during treatment.

Acute pyelonephritis, in 90 per cent of the instances, show an infection with a bacteria, *E. coli*, known to occur in about 2 per cent of the pregnant women. The usual route of infection is from the bladder and ureters to the kidneys.

High fever with chills and rigors, nausea, vomiting, low backache (usually at the junction of the spine with the lowermost rib) should arouse suspicion of this disease, particularly if the onset has been abrupt. Difficult micturition and slightly bloody urine may occur. Urine contains pus cells. Urine culture shows growth of the causative bacteria and helps in deciding about the chemotherapeutic agent.

Your doctor will prescribe drugs as soon as he is convinced of the diagnosis on urine examination. Later, chemotherapeutic agent may have to be changed if suggested by the culture-sensitivity report on urine. Take adequate bed rest during the acute phase.

As a general rule, pyelonephritis in pregnancy must not be regarded as cured unless and until repeated urine examinations reveal that urine is normal. Inadequate treatment may cause chronic *pyelonephritis* and *renal failure* in due course.

In a mild case of *chronic pyelonephritis*, the patient needs to be hospitalised. Incidence of intra-uterine death is 50 per cent. Those born alive are smaller in size. Many authorities advocate termination of pregnancy whereas others favour caesarean section at 38th week.

When the disease is severe, outlook for the mother as well as baby is very poor. It is safe to terminate the pregnancy.

Acute renal failure in pregnancy is an extremely serious condition. The output of urine becomes very, very small or nil. Such a woman should immediately be transferred to a good centre.

Intestinal parasitic infestations

Intestinal parasites are very common in developing countries and a leading cause of ill-health. When one or more of such parasites complicate a pregnancy, it becomes worse. Common parasites infesting Indian women are Entamoeba histolytica, Giardia lambia, H. nana (Dwarf tapeworm), hookworm, roundworm and threadworm.

The worst enemy of a pregnant woman is, however, hookworm. A large number of hookworms attach themselves firmly to the upper intestinal mucose, sucking blood. With heavy worm-load, significant anaemia occurs. The skin becomes pale, dry and muddy and the face puffy. Appetite is markedly decreased. The patient becomes lethargic and apathetic. Vague abdominal pain and palpitations are common. Ankle swelling (oedema) and breathlessness may occur.

Your doctor would like to have one or more stool examinations to confirm the presence of hookworm. Blood and sometime bone-marrow may also be tested.

Hookworm disease makes prognosis for the child as well as mother unfavourable. The mother may develop pre-eclamptic toxaemia and superimposed bacterial infections. In neglected cases, chances of abortion, premature birth and stillbirth are high.

Fortunately, it is easy to cure the disease. Very effective drugs are now available. Many obstetricians prefer giving anti-hookworm treatment as a routine in early months of pregnancy.

Mind you, the management of hookworm disease does not end with the administration of an anti-hookworm drug. You must follow the doctor's instructions regarding treatment of accompanying anaemia. If anaemia is mild to moderate, oral iron tablets will do. If it is severe, he may like to give you intravenous or intramuscular iron injection. At times it may become necessary to give a blood transfusion or two to raise haemoglobin speedily.

Heart disease

About 1 in 100 pregnant women may suffer from one or another heart disease. Most of such diseases have rheumatic origin, monopoly being that of mitral stenosis. The next group is congenital heart disease.

Every woman with a known heart disease must consult her doctor before rushing into pregnancy. Later, she should remain under strict antenatal care. What causes worst difficulties in such cases is development of heart failure. A major objective of antenatal check-up is to prevent it and, if that does not work, at least to diagnose it early so that prompt treatment can be given.

All pregnant women with heart disease should be hospitalised after 34th week in mild cases and 39th week in moderate to advanced cases. When failure is present, immediate hospitalisation, irrespective of the stage of pregnancy is recommended. It is practice on the part of obstetricians to manage such cases in consultation with a physician, preferably a cardiologist.

It is a common experience that complete bed rest, a few weeks before the expected date of delivery, goes a long way in ensuring relatively safe delivery at the time of labour. In most cases, normal vaginal delivery is considered the best.

Varicose veins

A common observation during later months of pregnancy is the development of prominent, enlarged and tortuous veins which protrude out of the skin. The so-called *varicose veins* are usually seen over the legs. Vulva, rectum, anus and vagina are the other sites.

Heredity is said to play a significant role in the development of varicosity. What seems a striking observation is that most of the women who develop it are the ones who stand or sit for long spans of time.

Among various causes of varicosity are rise in total amount of blood and greater intra-abdominal pressure in pregnancy.

To safeguard against varicosity, you are well advised to avoid standing for long hours during pregnancy. Try to sit with feet propped up every now and then. Lying down with feet raised also helps.

Once varicosity develops, it helps to wear elastic stockings.

In order to safeguard against varicosity in the rectum (the so-called *piles* or *haemorrhoids*) see that you do not have constipation. Take good deal of leafy vegetables and fruits.

Abortion

Abortion means termination of pregnancy before the "little life" in the womb is capable of viability which, as a rule, reaches at 28 weeks. Not all pregnancies, because of one or another reason, reach term successfully. It is estimated that in around 12 per cent cases abortion occurs.

If a pregnant woman has a slight abdominal pain (colicky), slight bleeding from the birth passage, frequency of micturition and backache, she appears to be heading for what is termed *threatened abortion.* The woman should immediately report to the doctor so that he can confirm the diagnosis and take remedial action. Generally speaking, complete bed rest is essential. Sedatives to relieve pain and anxiety are helpful. It will depend on your doctor's judgement whether he prescribes an oral or intramuscular hormonal preparation, *progesterone.*

Threatened abortion, if not taken care of, is likely to pass on to what is known as *inevitable* or *incomplete abortion.* Its diagnosis is suggested by the fact that pain becomes severer and vaginal bleeding more profuse. A part of products of conception may be protruding through the birth passage.

In most of the cases of inevitable abortion, products of conception are bound to be expelled spontaneously. In others, active interference by a doctor is indicated. The doctor will, under aspetic conditions and anaesthesia, evacuate the womb either digitally or by an instrument.

Missed abortion refers to the condition in which manifestations of abortion do appear but disappear soon. The products of conception—dead—are retained in the uterus. Abdominal pain and vaginal bleeding are more or less over. The blood in the uterus clots around this dead ovum which subsequently undergoes lots of changes. The doctor will evacuate the womb. But this should always be done in a hospital.

Therapeutic abortion means induction of planned abortion "in the interest of the mother".

Unfortunately many unscrupulous practitioners and the like are engaged in performing *criminal abortion* in the name of therapeutic abortion. This practice is responsible for a proportion of maternal mortality and morbidity.

5
CHILDBIRTH

Delivering a baby is a tough going, a hell of a lot of hard work. Hence its designation, *labour*. "The wonderful result the mother has at the end of it is worth all those pains," says Oscar Wilde. Let us have some insight into the whole process of childbirth.

Stages of labour

Arbitrarily the whole process of labour has been divided into three stages:

Stage 1: The earliest sign of labour is the occurrence of regular contractions of the womb. When these contractions become stronger, the woman feels these as *labour pains*. The neck of the womb, known as *cervix*, tends to dilate and the plug of mucus which closed its mouth comes off, letting some bloodstained discharge, *show*, leak out. This occurs during the relaxation period of the womb. During each contraction, which becomes more vigorous and more frequent with the passage of time, the muscles of the womb are busy pushing the baby's head against the cervix, thus helping contractions to stretch the cervix. Eventually, the mouth of the cervix is fully dilated.

Thus the interval between the onset of labour pains and the full dilatation of cervix (indicated by appearance of *show*) constitutes the first stage of labour. Its duration varies from 12 to 24 hours in primigravida and 4 to 12 hours in multigravida.

A word about recognition of labour pains. Do not confuse these with ordinary cramps. Labour pains, unlike cramps, come at regular intervals. To start with the pains come every 20 minutes. Later, the interval may be as small as 3 to 5 minutes.

Secondly, the pain starts in the back but then travels round to the front of the tummy.

Since the first stage lasts for ample time, there is usually little difficulty in transferring the woman to the hospital.

Stage 2: Once the cervix is fully dilated, the bag of water that surrounds the baby splits. There is thus a leakage of the fluid. At this point labour pains become very strong and the mother feels a pressing need to push the baby out. She should cooperate with the attending doctor, midwife and other staff by bearing down (tightening the abdominal muscles) during contractions. In between the pains she must relax.

Eventually, the baby's head reaches the vulva—the edge of the mother's body. The last push and the limbs and trunk are also born. As the body escapes, lots of blood-stained fluid (*liquir amnii*) also gushes out.

The second stage of labour thus begins with the complete dilatation of the cervix and ends with the birth of the baby. In multigravida it is a matter of some minutes, usually 15 minutes. The primigravida, on the other hand, may take an hour or two.

As soon as baby is expelled, the cord is clamped and cut.

Stage 3: After the birth of the baby, the mother relaxes. As the doctor is busy in clamping and cutting the cord, placenta, the so-called *after-birth,* is separating from its attachment to the womb. It takes about 10 minutes to do so.

As soon as there are signs indicating separation of the placenta (like lengthening of the cord, further leak of blood, womb becoming smaller, harder and more globular in shape and mobile from side to side), the woman expels it out by a voluntary effort. If the mother fails to cooperate after all that hard labour and exhaustion, pressing the woman's abdomen in a definite manner would push it out.

The third stage, therefore, lasts between the birth of the baby and expulsion of the placenta. It usually takes about 15 to 20 minutes and seldom more than half an hour. Once labour is over, the mother may have a rigor, *physiological chill*, which should be ignored.

About the baby just born, we will talk at length in the next section.

All about conduct of labour

Since labour concerns the pregnant woman primarily, she should have some idea how it is going to be conducted. Needless to say at the very outset that the process is completed more or less by nature. The role of the doctor and the midwife is described as "minimal interference". That cannot be said about the mother-to-be. Her contribution and role is very active indeed.

Preparation of the mother-to-be: The hair over external genitals are shaved off. A soap and water enema is given to evacuate the bowel so that she does not pass stools during labour pains. It is good to have a bath before entering the labour room.

The attending doctor would like to have obstetric examination, including vaginal examination, to ascertain certain information.

In the *first stage*, maternal condition, pulse and temperature are recorded every 4 hourly. The foetal heart rate is also recorded every 4 hourly. The progress of labour is assessed from the relationship of foetal head to the brim of the pelvis.

In this stage the woman is allowed to walk about. But as pains become frequent and strong, she should be put to bed. Mild sedatives and tranquillizers may be given to her. Avoid ingesting solids but there is no harm in taking small amounts of liquid food at intervals.

No sooner does the second stage begin, it is made sure that she passes urine and the bladder is fully emptied. If she fails to do that, doctors would like to put a catheter in her urethra.

As the second stage progresses, she is placed in the dorsal position. Now is the time for the woman to hold her breath and contract her abdominal muscle (the so-called *bearing-down*) during the pains and never in between.

Once rupture of membranous bag containing watery fluid in which the baby floats has ruptured, baby's heartbeat is recorded every 15 minutes.

As the head of the baby presses against the perineum and the anus dilates, the doctor takes action to prevent very fast expulsion of the head. This he does by promoting its flexion and encouraging its delivery not during contractions but in between them. The woman should not bear down at this point. Instead she should relax, open her mouth and breathe deeply. The doctor may like to give her a light anaesthetic to relax her.

All this helps to prevent perineal laceration, which generally shows poor healing. Most obstetricians, however take an additional precaution as well. They perform a planned surgical incision (usually mediolateral) in the perineal floor in all primigravida. This cut is known as *episiotomy* and is sutured carefully afer the expulsion of the placenta at a later point. The whole procedure should be carried out under strict aseptic conditions.

As soon as the baby's head is born, separate soft linen pieces are used to clean the eyes while a piece of gauze is used to clean the lips and nose. Mucus from the mouth is best aspirated.

After the birth of the head, the woman bears down in the next contraction to deliver the shoulders while the doctor applies gentle traction upward for the posterior and downward for the anterior shoulder.

Once shoulders are out, spontaneous delivery of the baby is a rule. The baby should be allowed to cry vigorously. This may need little compression of the chest or a banging of the feet. No delay should occur in clearing air passages by aspiration.

TABLE
Apgar Score of the Newborn

Feature		Score	
	0	1	2
A Appearance pink(colour)	Blue; pale	Body pink; limbs blue	Fully
P Pulse (heart rate)	Absent	Below 100/min	Over 100/min
G Grimace (reflex irritability after stimulation of sole of foot)	Absent	Present	Cry
A Activity (muscle tone)	Absent	Some flexion of limbs	Good active movements
R Respiration	Absent	Slow; irregular	Good strong cry

At this stage, the doctor evaluates the 1-minute Apgar score to find out if resuscitation is indicated.

The cord is held at the vulval outlet between the index finger and the thumb. When it stops pulsating, a ligature is placed about an inch from the baby's umblicus and another closest to the vulva. The cord is now divided as close to the umblical ligature as possible. After cutting the cord with scissors, the stump is dressed after making sure that no blood is oozing.

While expulsion of placenta is being awaited in the third stage, the doctor re-examines the perineum in good light, noting not only the superficial but also the deep lacerations, if any.

Once the placenta and membranes are expelled, these are carefully examined for any retained portions inside the womb which may cause bleeding and sepsis later.

Lastly, episiotomy cuts as also any laceration are carefully sutured.

All said and done, the woman is carefully cleansed. A sterile gauze is applied to the vulva and fixed. It is changed as often as it becomes soiled. To provide comfort to the woman an abdominal binder is usually applied. She is, as a rule, kept under observations for at least one hour after completion of the third stage in the labour room per se.

Some women keep getting *after-pains* over quite a few days after the birth of the baby. These pains stimulate the cramps experienced during menstrual periods. The doctor would prescribe a pain-killer which helps.

Childbirth is not always smooth sailing

The childbirth is a process beset with many hazards and problems. Yet, most healthy mothers who had careful antenatal check-up do have successful outcome of pregnancy and labour. That is not to say childbirth is always a smooth sailing. Far from it!

Why does childbirth become "difficult" at times? The causes are quite a few. In the first place, the lie of the foetus may be abnormal—head up rather than the normal head down position. This is called *breech presentation*. Secondly, contractions of the womb may not be adequate. Thirdly, outlet of the pelvis may be too small to permit an easy passage of the baby at labour. Fourthly, more than one foetus in the womb (*multiple births*) may create difficulties during birth. Fifthly, the mother may find herself unable to push the baby out.

Breech presentation refers to a "head up, buttocks down" baby in the womb. Doctors do diagnose it during antenatal and generally succeed in correcting the presentation by manipulation as such or under anaesthesia.

When manipulation fails, doctors are left with no way out but to deliver the baby bottom first. And that is a tough job.

Birth dangers to the baby

The baby, as you would appreciate, is subjected to quite a few stresses and strains, which could well be hazardous, during the birth process. The risk of hazards multiplies in the presence of congenital defects, low-birth weight, difficult deliveries and complicated pregnancy which may affect the foetus in some form or the other.

Yet, it is a wonder of wonders that the vast majority of the babies are born normally. Hats off to the advances made by the medical science over the years! And, salutation to Nature for doing still greater!

In the first place, during labour, as and when there is a labour pain, which implies that the womb is contracting, the baby is deprived of its blood supply and thus his oxygen. His ability to bear this oxygen deprivation temporarily is unique. As soon as the relaxation phase begins he breathes again. Once in a while, it may so happen that oxygen deprivation becomes far too much and lasts far too long. In such a situation, he may suffer from a brain damage. It is possible that the so-called "child with *minimal brain dysfunction*" who is slow to learn, dull and clumsy, has had difficult or delayed birth leading to oxygen deprivation and somewhat damaged brain.

Secondly, the relatively large head of the baby may undergo far too much of squeezing and *moulding* during its passage through the narrow birth canal. Excessive stress and pressure on the soft tissue of the brain and its covering membranes may cause tearing, laceration and bleeding into the brain. The result will be a *permanent brain damage*.

Also during passage through the very narrow birth canal, the shoulders—the next largest part of the baby—squeezing during contraction of the womb may cause fractures of the bones in and around the shoulder joint.

Not all deliveries are conducted in a natural way. At times it becomes necessary to apply attractive and fascinating instruments called *forceps* to assist in the delivery while some babies get born through a surgical opening made in the abdominal wall and the womb, the so-called *caesarean section.* Such intervention is usually required when the lie of the baby is not normal, the birth passage is far too narrow, the contractions of the womb are inadequate or some such thing. Though instruments are always applied very carefully, a little risk of damage to head or a fracture is always there.

Sometime it happens that a baby with a tendency to bleed may show blood oozing from the umblical stump or from elsewhere. He may bleed spontaneously from the gut. Bleeding from the gut may present as blood in the motion or the vomitus. A prompt management is indicated.

Last but not least, the baby may not be able to breathe and cry at all or for a considerable time even after birth. This is bound to either cause a failure on the part of various physiological processes to begin or to damage some of these a great lot.

6

THE "LABOUR OF LOVE" IS HERE

So, at long last, the "little stranger"—your "labour of love"—has arrived. He has just said goodbye to the comforts of the warm, watery world. With the very first breath and the cry, his struggle in adjusting to the airy world begins. A large majority of these adjustments to an independent life is achieved during the very first week of life or a little later.

Looking at him: his appearance

Do not raise eyebrows if the *new arrival* does not exactly turn out to be what you had anticipated or fancied. In the first place, you perhaps wanted to have a boy whereas you got a girl. Or, maybe you got a daughter instead of a son. Remember, it's all Nature's doing. We cannot do a thing about it. Or, can we? Secondly, you perhaps imagined the "little one"would resemble quite a lot the babies depicted on the picture postcards, glossy advertisements or calendars. Your baby, on the contrary, looks odd with a large head, dome-shaped abdomen, lean and thin buttocks and the skin covered with a waxy material. He looks more of a little monkey. And, that is quite a contrast to the picture in your mind—a lovely, chubby infant who would start playing with you as soon as he gets born. Wait, another 3 or 4 months and he will in all probability start conforming to your fancied picture. All that you have to do is to give him ample love and bring him up properly.

Let us have some details of how the newborn looks.

Skin: The skin is covered with a yellowish-white, greasy (cheese-like) material called *vernix caseosa.* It was a natural protective covering to safeguard his skin while lying in the water-bag within the mother's womb. After birth, it need not be removed when the baby is cleaned. Let it be there for sometime. It will wash off with the first bath.

If vernix is stained yellow, your doctor will notice it and act promptly to exclude *haemolytic disease of the newborn*. Incompatibility between mother's and baby's blood groups is responsible for this disease.

Once vernix peels off, the underlying skin shows up quite red and rather raw. Some desquamation of the skin may also occur, making the raw areas and minor abrasions susceptible to a bacterial infection.

At places, particularly over the buttocks, you may find large bluish spots. These are the *monogolian spots* which have no significance and will disappear in due course—yes, on their own.

"Will my baby continue to be as fair as he seems right away?"—this is an oft-asked question. Remember, absence of enough pigment, *melanin*, is responsible for baby's extra-fair colour at birth. In some weeks it is going to darken as the normal development of the pigment occurs.

Head: Compared to the body it is large and rather odd-looking because of the overriding and moulding it underwent during the birth process. This odd shape need not panic you. In a few days the head will assume its normal rounded appearance. On your part, see that you keep changing its position as the baby is asleep. This will provide the head uniform pressure on all sides and assist it in resuming its normal shape.

At times you may find a soft swelling over the area of the head which got born first. It is very transitory and will last no longer than a couple of days. It is termed *caput succedaneum*.

In some babies, one or two longer-lasting swellings may be seen on top of the head. The so-called *cephalhaematoma* results from stretching of the veins of the scalp before or during birth and is quite harmless. Do not run from quack to quack in pursuit of its treatment. Listen to your doctor. It needs no treatment and usually disappears within 2 or 3 months.

Talking about the mechanical effects on the head—well, the baby may show marks or swelling over the head if forceps had been applied during delivery. Do not bother about these. Their disappearance occurs very fast.

If you run your hand over the head, you will find that bones of the skull are separated from each other by slight gaps called *sutures*. If you examine the front of the skull, a large gap (diamond-shaped and measuring 3 x 2 cm.) at a point where the bones do not meet is very striking. This is known as *anterior fontanelle*. It is an important landmark, giving very useful information to the doctors. It usually closes between 9 and 18 months of age.

Similarly at the back is a much smaller gap, called posterior fontanelle which usually closes by the age of 2 months or so. Doctors do not attach as much importance to it as to the anterior one.

Grandmothers are usually fond of putting some vague substance and oily things over the anterior fontanelle ("this will make the child brainy and keep him cool"). Avoid all that. For, that will only lead to accumulation of dirt and formation of a dirty crust over the head.

Hair: Most babies are born with lots of hair on the head. In some, especially in case of prematurity, hair grows down the back of the neck and across the shoulders. This hair is known as *lanugo*. It will fall off soon.

Hair on the scalp may also fall off during the first few weeks. This should not be confused with baldness. Hair will regrow. I have come across numerous babies in whom type and colour of hair at this second growth is characteristically different from that of the hair seen at birth.

Eyes: The baby at birth keeps the eyes closed most of the time. All newborns have blue eyes but after the first month change in colour may begin to occur. It will be difficult to predict true permanent colour of the eyes until baby is at least 9 months of age.

Do not be upset if the baby gives an impression of *cross-eye*, also called *strabismus* or *squint*. It is because of lack of coordination between the eye muscles. It is all normal for a newborn and for several later months.

The baby is capable of differentiating between darkness and light.

Mouth: Just because the baby does not move his tongue quite a lot, do not get into your head the idea that he is what is known as *tongue-tied* and run about wild to get it cut. The condition is rare and, in any case, needs no interference until the age of 3 years. It does not cause speech defects as is commonly but erroneously held by folklore.

You may find pale grey-coloured areas on the roof of the mouth or close to the palate and on the inner surface of the lips. These help the baby to fix his lips tightly around the mother's nipple during breast-feeding.

Once in a while, a newborn may show eruption of one or two teeth. It is foolish to ascribe superstition to such a benign and harmless thing. Put your foot down if the elders insist on seeking service of *witchcraft*.

Abdomen: The newborn's belly is round and full, more so after a feed when it feels like a tight little drum. This is perfectly normal.

The stump of the navel does look very odd but there is no way out. In any case its life is short. It begins to dry up within 24 hours. It will drop off after 5 to 10 days. What it is going to leave as a reminder is the wrinkled "button", which when inverted will become the so-called navel or umblicus—something all of us have. Never pull off the umblical stump; it will bleed, inviting troubles. Let it fall off on its own.

Breasts: Every other newborn has a swollen breast; even a drop of milk may appear from the nipples. This is the same substance as secreted by the mother and is, in fact, the result of the mother's hormones passing into the baby's blood while inside the womb. The swelling and secretion will stop after a few weeks. Make no attempt to squeeze the breasts.

Likewise, some female newborns may have a slight discharge as such or somewhat bloodstained from the vagina a few days following the birth. This again needs no treatment.

In a full-term newborn, the breast nodule measures 5 to 7 mm. If the baby is born before 36 weeks of gestation, its diameters will be just 3 mm. Before a gestation of 33 weeks, it is simply not palpable.

External genitals: The foreskin over the tip of the penis may be tightly overriding the hole through which urine passes, making the latter very tight. This causes difficulty in passing urine. Your doctor may like to give a little surgical cut and correct the minor defect. In case it is gross, the so-called *phimosis*, the baby may need a small operation in which the foreskin is snipped and pushed back. This is called *circumcision*. In certain communities, say Mohammedans and Jews, it is performed in each and every child as a "ritual".

In some babies, testicles, the organs which will be responsible for production of sperms in later life, are not palpable in the bag of skin behind the penis, the *scrotum*. Doctors usually do nothing about this problem at this stage. They follow the baby. In many cases, testicles do descend within a month; in others they may take longer. Usually if the testicles have not descended by 3 years of age, a hormonal or surgical treatment is carried out.

You may find that the scrotum is quite enlarged. Your doctor will be able to tell you if it is hernia, hydrocele or just normal.

Measurements: On an average a newborn in the Western countries weighs about 3.4 kg., though the variation is considerable.

An average newborn in India and other Asian countries weighs less. Your doctor will give the baby special care in case he is less than 2.5 kgs. He may need to be kept in an *incubator*, a temperature regulated apparatus in which low birth weight babies can be reared.

In the first 7 days after birth, most newborns lose 10 per cent of the birth weight. By the 10th day weight loss is regained. After that a healthy infant gains about 200 gms every week.

The average length of a newborn baby is around 50 cm, most babies falling in the range 45 to 53 cm.

The average circumference of head is about 35 cm.

Most mothers would be interested in knowing if all low birth weight babies will grow up to be dull, small and delicate and all hefty newborns to be strong and big. The answer is a plain "no". Some "big shots", including Sir Isaac Newton, Sir Winston Churchill and Nobel Laureate Rabindranath Tagore, were born small enough at birth to be "put in a big coat pocket". Likewise, some big babies at birth have ended up in later years as very small and delicate.

Remember, size at birth has less to do with the eventual outcome; your care has more.

His behaviour and performance

Certain reflexes: If you place an object in his hand, it is at once grasped around fairly firmly. Try your fingers, one for each of his hands. Once he has held these tightly, you can hold him suspended in the air. This is called *grasp reflex.*

If you touch the angle of his mouth with your finger, he will immediately turn his head to that side. He will also open his mouth and push his tongue over to the corner of the mouth. This is what is termed *rooting reflex.* It helps him to root for the nipple and find it during breast-feeding.

If you hold the baby under the arm, raised and made to touch his foot to the edge of a table, he will curl the foot up, raise it and place it on the table. This is called *placing reflex.*

If you put the flat of the newborn's foot on a table, he will lift the other foot as well as though he was walking. This is the *walking reflex.*

On sudden banging of the table on which the newborn is lying awake, he will at once throw out his hands and fingers wide open, pull his legs up and cry. This is followed by his pulling the arms together in a "close embrace". This is the *Moro's reflex*.

When doctors are not certain about a mother's statement about the duration of pregnancy, they can judge the newborn's approximate gestational age from these and other reflexes. So, do not look at the doctor working on eliciting reflexes in your baby with the curiosity of the little girl in *Alice in Wonderland*.

Activity: Incoordinate movements of the arms and legs, when he is lying on his back, occur in the newborn as and when he is awake.

Sleep and wakefulness: The baby sleeps a lot, waking up periodically, usually to receive the feed. In the latter half of each span of "sleeping hours", his sleep is quite deep and he cannot be easily aroused.

Bladder: Do not be panicky if he does not pass urine for 24 to 36 hours. It is not that his kidneys are not yet functioning. They are. What is contributing to delay in passing urine is the failure on the part of the bladder to empty it.

Bowel: It is different with the bowel. He usually passes his first stool right at birth or sometime during the first 24 hours.

The first stool is black, causing a good deal of staining of the diaper. It is called *meconium*. In the subsequent bowel movements, especially after 3 days, black meconium changes colour to brown and then to yellow. The sooner you put him to the breast, the faster the meconium gives way to real stools.

Crying: The first thing the newborn learns is to cry. It comes with the very first breath. It is an important means to attract the mother's attention and to express himself.

You can read a lot in a newborn's "cry". If it is choked and gasping (which one does encounter immediately after birth), the baby may be having a breathing difficulty. Its absence in toto indicates extreme distress. A high-pitched, shrill cry resembling the mewing of a cat may mean brain damage.

Feeding: The healthy newborn can suck and swallow well. As I hinted earlier, he nearly masters sucking while in the womb and is well trained after getting born. He is also trained to swallow and digest his natural food, mother's milk. His body too is trained to utilise it for its growth.

The average baby needs to be fed 6 to 8 times everyday, taking 90 to 100 ml of milk at every sitting.

Colostrum, the thick yellow milk produced by the mother during the first 2 or 3 days after childbirth, is ideal food for the newborn. It is in fact tailored to his needs. You are advised to let it be fed to the baby. There is nothing more stupid than to say that colostrum will harm the baby. Make sure you give it to the baby rather than being getting "trapped" in loose and baseless misstatements.

Other behaviours: All newborns have hiccoughs, sneezes, and yawns. Do not fuss that he has indigestion or wind, a cold or tiredness. These reactions do not mean anything. Nearly all babies have each one of these. None of these appears to do any harm to him.

Likewise, your baby's jaw may show "trembling" from time to time. This too has no special behavioural importance. A few years back, I had a tough time convincing an anxious mother about the benign nature of "trembling" that her few-days-old baby exhibited. I had to talk to her mother. It was only when the mother of the young lady emphatically told her "O, yes, you too used to have this kind of trembling when you were very small and we had to do nothing for it" that she was satisfied.

Again, the newborn gives a sudden jerk as and when there is sudden noise, a sudden change in his position or when his bedclothes are moved. Ignore it.

A proportion of the newborns develop high fever on second or third day after birth. The baby seems fine. His tongue and mouth are, however, dry. It is ascribed to the weight loss experienced by nearly every newborn and is termed *dehydration fever*. Do not panic about it: it does not mean an infection. All that you are supposed to do is to give plenty of boiled water in between the feeds. If fever is too high, you may give paracetamol. Do ask your doctor as to when to give it and in how much dose. Self-medication can prove dangerous, especially when it is the case of a newborn.

Lastly, a newborn can feel pain, thirst, hunger, heat and cold. Not just that. He can have happiness and anxiety. He is a person who can think about them.

As a mother you must understand his deepest emotional needs. Your concern should not be just his physical body. You must take care of the little one's mind—his behaviour and his emotional states—as well.

7

TAKING CARE OF THE NEWBORN

Let me begin by recalling the glaring features of the "care" immediately after the baby is born.

The aim of care at birth is that the baby's basic needs i.e., establishing breathing, adequate nutrition, body temperature and avoiding contact with infection, are met. Also, it will be important to help him in adjusting to the new life outside the mother's womb.

As soon as he is born, the doctor or the midwife suspends him by the feet (head downward) to drain blood and fluid from his nose, mouth and stomach. The 1-minute Apgar score is taken.

Before cutting the cord, it is made certain that it had stopped pulsating. Then, the operator milks it towards the infant. In this way the infant gets about 100 ml of additional blood. This will stand him in good stead afterwards. It is advisable to make a note of the blood vessels in the cord. A single artery is usually associated with some congenital malformations.

Having made a careful survey of the newborn's body for any congenital defect, the operator records the 5-minute Apgar score.

If the mother is conscious, it will be a good idea to let her handle the baby at this stage. She may also feel like putting him to the breast. Most authorities, as a matter of fact, encourage such an attitude. There is a good deal of evidence that such a policy goes a long way in establishing a healthy mother-child relationship and successful breast-feeding.

The right place to sleep

Though there is no hard and fast rule, it is a distinct advantage to place the baby in a pre-warmed cot to sleep. This cot should be kept by the mother's bedside so that she can cuddle, fondle and feed him as and when needed. Watching the baby sleep and awake under her very nose gives her immense contentment. Experience has demonstrated that if the mother and the baby share the same bed, accidental deaths (by way of the baby getting suffocated under the weight of the sleeping mother) may occur.

The so-called *nursery* in the obstetric unit of a hospital is not the right place for a healthy newborn. It is meant for the sick, the low-birth-weight and pre-term babies.

Bathing the baby: when and how?

In the good-old days it was virtually a "ritual" to bathe the newborn immediately after birth, almost always within the first 2 hours. Today, we know that it is of advantage not to bathe a newborn during the first week. For one, it helps to keep infection at arm's length. In fact, the number of maternity units where no bath is given until the baby is past 7 days has been on the increase.

What I am trying to say is that "dip bath" should be avoided until the cord sheds off. That, however, should not be interpreted as meaning that the new born should not be cleaned or sponged. The fact is that the baby has got to be kept clean by sponging gently. Special attention should be paid to the diaper area and the creases. You should, however, take a precaution not to rub off the protective cheeselike covering on his skin, the *vernix caseosa*.

Once the cord has separated, you may begin to give him a "dip bath" everyday. Make sure that you do not use a soap containing hexachlorophene which is said to be absorbed through the baby's skin and to be toxic to the nervous system.

It is not a bad idea to give the baby a gentle massage with olive oil, coconut oil, mustard oil or any good proprietary baby oil, before he takes the bath. It will help to keep his skin healthy and soft.

How should the baby be bathed? This is an oft-asked question by inexperienced mothers.

A colourful baby bathtub or a basin makes an excellent equipment to bathe the newborn. Before making a start, make sure that you have around the corner everything that you will need while giving him a bath. Also see that the water in the mini-tub or the basin is just lukewarm. Remember it should be "elbow-warm" and not "hand-warm." The latter will be too hot to be tolerated by the delicate baby. Also, make sure that the room in which you propose to give the baby the bath is warm enough and free of excessive air or wind. Remove wristwatch, rings or jewellery around your wrist or forearm.

Now sit before the bath of comfortably warm water and either spread a towel over your lap or wear an apron. Hold the undressed baby, giving the head a little dip. Apply a small quantity of a baby shampoo to the scalp. Rub it well. Then rinse off. Dry the head gently with a towel. Make sure that you do not press the fontanellae too hard and that you do not let soapy cloth touch the eyes. Use a fresh swab of cotton wool for wiping each eye. With separate swabs clean areas around nose, ears and folds at the surface of ears. Do not poke bits of cotton within the ears or nostrils.

Now is the time to soap the baby all over with your hand, allowing the head to rest on your forearm. As soon as you lower him gently into the water, the soap will wash off. You may rub his skin or splash water over him. Do not worry when he kicks in the water.

You may now lift him up and dry his body with a clean towel. Do not forget to clean the elbows, buttocks, knees, neck and genitals.

Next, powder his body, not directly but by first rubbing it on your hand. Mind you, if breathed into the baby's nostrils, the powder can prove harmful. Also, even the best of baby powders can cause discomfort by collecting in skin creases, especially in summer.

The stage is all set now to dress our "little friend" up. Put on the nappie first and then the plastic pants. In Section 8 are given details about nappies.

Now, you may slip over the vest (at the crown of head) followed by the top clothes.

Clothing

Remember, the newborn has got to be kept rather warm, but not too warm. His garments should not make him sweat. Unfortunately, overclothing is practised far too frequently, covering the baby with layers and layers of woollies even in good weather. That is undesirable. Such babies do not suck well, become drowsy and show failure to thrive, developing constipation and *prickly heat* rash.

Also avoid woollies touching the neck of the baby. An annoying rash may result.

During summer, all that may suffice for the baby is a vest and a nappie.

Care of the umblical stump

As was pointed out earlier, the umblical stump after the birth of the baby is usually touched with an antibacterial agent and sometimes dressed by the attending doctor in the labour room *per se*.

As a rule the stump will fall off in a week's time provided it is left as such and neither made wet by a bath nor pulled out. If, on shrivelling, the stump leaves behind a little scabby area, apply a baby cream to it every-day.

At times, pus or a watery discharge may ooze out from the umblicus. Sometimes, you may find, when the baby is 2 or 3 week old, a pea-size mass buried in it. This is called *polyp* or *granulation*. A doctor's opinion should be sought in such a situation. Remember, a septic umblicus can spread infection to the rest of the body. The disease thus produced, *septicaemia*, is serious and can prove fatal.

Bad hygiene and neglect of the umblicus can lead to another killing disease, *tetanus*. It is almost always seen in babies delivered and cared for in traditional ways and means. Mind you, one cause of tetanus in the newborn is the application of dust. cowdung or traditional pastes.

Care of the nose

It is important to keep the nose clean. Else, a blocked nose may cause undue crying and breathing difficulty. Avoid poking cotton wool plugs into the nose. Not infrequently I have seen little babies brought for "crying to death" and a peep into the nostrils reveals a tiny cotton piece plugging the air passage. So, remember, good "mothering" also includes attention to such small things.

Care of the eyes and ears

The ears and eyes should be cleaned at every bath as underscored earlier in this section.

Do not get into the habit of pouring warm oil into his ear canals. You will only be boosting accumulation of more wax rather than getting rid of it.

Also, when you clean his eyes, see that you move the cotton swab or the edge of the towel from the corner, close to the nose towards the outer side. Do not put kajal or surma in his eyes.

Care of the fingernails

You need to attend to your baby's fingernails as carefully as yours. Keep them short; they may require cutting every 3 or 4 days. Else he may have ulcers in his mouth and sores over the skin.

When to take him outdoors

Recently, I overheard the mother of an overprotected 2-month old, priding in telling a host of women, "It's the first time I have exposed him to the world outside our cosy room." That is a wrong attitude.

You should begin to put your baby, once he is a week old, outdoors for an hour or two everyday provided that the weather is conducive. Dress him adequatly—neither too much nor too little. Just that he is going to stay out for his daytime nap(s) is not a good reason to wrap him with too many clothes.

In order that he gets used to the sun, do expose him to sunlight. Avoid the glare of the sun falling on his eyes, however.

Paediatric check-up

Do not wait for a medical problem to knock but have him examined by a specialist. Look up the doctor for his first paediatric check-up when he is one month old. During the first year of life, it is advisable to have him regularly checked every month or so. Put your difficulties and queries over to the doctor.

Care of the skin

Much of what I would like to say here has already been said. So, let me be a little choosy.

I had stressed the need for a daily bath. On hot days, it may become necessary to have an additional bath in the afternoon.

After giving the bath, see that you do not rub his delicate skin with a towel. Rather, pat it with a soft, dry towel.

Do not leave the baby for any length of time, "cooling his heels", with a soiled or wet nappy. Else he may develop what is known as *nappy rash*.

Also, do not rub the stool off his buttocks while changing the nappie. Instead, use cotton wool dipped in olive oil or wash his bottom with warm water.

Play

Once the baby is a week or two old, he should be put in a pram after his morning feed or afterwards. The mother should find time to play with him. Even newborns enjoy playing.

If you are going to keep him in the pram in the greenery of your lawn, make sure you have him protected from mosquitoes and other insects. A mosquito net may be required.

Sleep

As I said earlier the newborn sleeps nearly all through day and night but for the feeding periods. It is estimated that he sleeps for almost 22 hours a day.

There is nothing wrong in this sleep pattern. In fact the time-honoured belief that "children grow in their sleep" is well founded. When the ligaments are relaxed during sleep, the chance of growth in length increases.

Mothers and elders in the family often feel disturbed when the baby gets into the habit of sleeping prone. Remember, it is normal for a newborn and a little older infant to sleep on his abdomen. In fact, it is safer and more comfortable for the baby. You may well encourage him to do so.

As pointed out at the outset of this section, you should let your newborn sleep in a baby cot or crib by your bedside rather than have him share your bed. There are several types of cradles available in the market. You may buy a collapsible one. It is fairly economical. Also, since it is folding, no space problem is posed. It would keep serving your baby for some 2 or 3 years.

Using the thermometer

Forget the "rectal temperature". The procedure is risky and, unless you are an expert (forgive me if you are!), it may hurt the rectum, the lowermost end of the gut that opens into the anus.

Also forget the "mouth temperature" when it concerns the newborn or a little older baby.

The armpit (axilla) or the groin is the right place for you to record a baby's temperature. What is highly important is to remember to keep the thermometer in place for at least 3 minutes. The so-called "half minute" and instant thermometers are misnomers.

Vaccination

We shall discuss the subject of protection against infections through immunisation (vaccination) at length in Section 16.

BCG vaccination has come under a cloud following the much publicised Chingleput study. A National Workshop held under the aegis of the Indian Academy of Paediatrics, has recommended its continuation. The workshop has called for concerted research to evaluate whether BCG gives protection against childhood tuberculosis or not.

You, as the mother of the "little one", should not do anything just because the lay press has said so. You must get your child the BCG vaccination as soon as possible after birth. There is plenty of evidence that it protects, and absolutely none, that it does not, as far as children are concerned. Mind you, the much-talked-about Chingleput study concerned the adults. Children are not the same as adults.

8

MORE ABOUT NAPPIES AND CLOTHING

A good mother must give adequate attention to the newborn's clothing with special reference to *diapers* or *napkins*, popularly known as *nappies*. Do not leave all this to the care of the *ayah*. She may be very good but she is unlikely to be a perfect substitute for your personal touch, understanding and care.

You have been purely misled if you are under the impression that the baby's clothing care is a tedious job. It is not. With good planning and thoughtfulness, it is very much simple. It is also "rewarding" when you think of it in terms of the infant's health and protection against infections.

Nappies

I know of two types available in our set-up. First, cotton fabric nappies which are washable and ready for use again and again. The second type is the readymade disposable and sterile, available from sophisticated markets. I would leave the choice to you. You can use any of the two depending on your circumstances. If you opt for the first one, see that you buy soft but durable stuff. Frequent laundering will be possible only then.

How to fold a nappie: There are 4 ways: First is the *triangle nappie*. Here, fold the nappie into a triangle. Then, put the triangle under baby's buttocks. One corner should lie between his legs. The other two corners should lie round the baby's middle. Join the three corners with a safety pin in the front.

Second is the *oblong nappie* in which there are two ends at the back. You should bring the corner of the front up between the legs and then join to the ends of the back with safety pins.

Third, the so-called *twisted nappie* is more or less the same as an oblong nappie. But you are required to twist it before bringing up between the legs and then join the ends of the back to the ends of the front with safety pins.

In the fourth type, *kite nappie*, the sides of the nappie are so folded that it becomes wide on the top and narrow at the bottom. Using safety pins, join the front and the back ends.

Use of safety pins: Exercise due care when you put in the pin. Slip two fingers of your hand between the nappie and the baby's skin so that the pin does not prick him. Also see that you buy good quality pins, the ones which do not open on their own. Thirdly, ensure that the sharp end of the safety pin is away from the infant's body. All these precautions will help you to prevent accidental hurt to the baby.

When to change the nappie: You must change the nappie as soon as you know it is soiled. An exceptional baby may not care if he is wet but most of them do become restless and cry. I may sound to be repeating but do not ever rub the infant's buttocks with the nappie. Rather wash it or clean it with cotton soaked in a baby oil. Do not forget to make the area dry, sprinkle powder on it before putting on another nappie.

Remember, too, it is a good habit to change the nappie before and after each and every feeding session. If you are highly overworked, even then it will be advisable to find time to change his nappie either before you pick him up for feeding or after it.

Nappie washing: Before beginning to wash, remove the loose stools from the dirty nappies in the toilet by scraping or rinsing it in the flush. It is a good idea to put the used diapers or nappies in a basin containing water and soap or detergent.

It is not necessary to wash the nappies in a special washing machine. A wash tub containing water and soap or a detergent will suffice. Repeat rinsings until the water becomes clear. Usually, two rinsings suffice.

As an extra precaution, the thus-washed nappies may now be put in the Dettol solution for some 20 to 30 minutes. Squeeze the water out, let the nappies dry and finally iron them. The use of Dettol helps to prevent occurrence of the so-called *nappie* or *diaper rash*, a troublesome problem in some babies.

Diaper liners—yes or no?: The paper or treated cloth-made, if available, are certainly of help in protecting the nappie from getting wet. These are placed between baby's skin and the nappie. There is no truth in the saying that these may harm the baby. These are of special help during travelling.

Protective pants—yes or No?: These again are of very special help when you are travelling with the baby. They should not be too tight, should not be used in the presence of nappie rash, should be replaced frequently and should be sterilised in the same way as nappies.

These pants are waterproof, made of either rubber or plastic.

Clothes

If you wish to make an easy go of it—yes, both for the baby and for your ownself—remember, your baby is going to grow incredibly fast and will before long outgrow his present clothes. Also, mind you, his skin is soft and may respond adversely to anything that tends to irritate it.

That is why the clothes which you make for your baby should be soft, comfortable, fairly loose, easy-to-wear, attractive and easily washable. And, do not make too many of these just to satisfy your "ego". Also, remember to avoid pleats, fussy frills, buttons and zippers which may poke the baby.

It is always most comfortable for the baby to have a cotton vest next to his skin. Nylon or any other synthetic vest is not recommended. Do not use tight elastic in panties, socks or sleeves. It may cause tummy pain or swelling of the foot or hand.

The baby need not be overclothed. All that he needs is a little more than what is comfortable for you. If you are okay with a thick cardigan, the baby will perhaps need a light sweater as well. Do not wrap him in one or two vests, one or two shirts, two or three sweaters and a cardigan or a coat. That will be far too much even in a severe cold.

Make sure that the wool you use for his sweater etc. is very soft and of very fine quality. Avoid its direct contact with the skin, especially that of the neck. It will be a good idea to put a *bib* around the infant's neck. It will protect against direct contact as also prevent soiling of the woolly when the child urinates.

9

THE LOW-BIRTH-WEIGHT BABY

So far we have been talking about more or less the healthy full-term babies. Unfortunately, a significant proportion (33 per cent) of the babies born in the Asian countries are low birth weight, either as a result of growth retardation of the foetus or due to birth much before the expected date of delivery. In the first case, the baby is termed *small for dates* (weight low compared to the gestational age) and in the second he is designated as *preterm* or *premature*.

According to WHO, a newborn with a birth weight of 2.5 kgs. ($5^1/_2$ lb) or less (irrespective of the period of gestation) is classified as a *low-birth-weight baby*. He needs extra care.

Experience in the developing countries (and that includes India) shows that babies with weight between 2000 gms. and 2,500 gms. often possess good potential for growth and health and may be managed as we manage normal newborns. Somewhat extra care will, however, be of advantage to them.

The newborns weighing less than 2,000 gms. are, however, *high risk babies*. They are highly vulnerable and both anatomically as well as functionally immature. Mortality is high in this category of babies. They are the candidates for intensive care in the so-called *Nursery*, within the maternity unit. Remember, in order to protect the inmates against infection, visitors are not allowed to the Nursery. The mother, too, stays a little away in the adjoining room.

How he looks

The baby is small in size; the head looks very large for his tiny body. The face looks small, buccal pad of fat is absent and eyes are protruding. Ear cartilage is either absent or deficient.

Hair is fuzzy and woolly with profuse *lanugo* over the body. The cheese-like skin covering, *vernix*, is scanty. Also, the skin has little subcutaneous fat, looks thin and excessively pink. Deep sole creases and breast nodule are absent.

Scrotum is underdeveloped. Testicles are not found in it. In baby girls, clitoris is hypertrophied and labia minora is prominently visible.

His reflexes are poor; so is his general activity.

Handicaps

The smaller the baby, the weaker is his hold on life.

The immaturity of his brain leads to poor activity and lethargy. Breathing difficulties may cause *blue spells*. Your doctor may need to resuscitate him.

His temperature-regulatory mechanism is inadequate. Subnormal temperature (hypothermia) is seen in a large majority of such babies and may prove fatal. At times, he may develop high fever (*hyperthermia*) too.

Incoordination in sucking and swallowing causes vomiting and choking. The capacity of the stomach is small and he can tolerate only very small amounts of feeds. Digestive upsets are common. As a result of poor tone of the muscles, abdominal distension is common.

Since liver enzymes are rather immature in such a baby, blood bilirubin level is relatively high and stays high for a prolonged time. This will be apparent to the mother as a prolongation of the so-called *physiological jaundice* over a longer period. Also, high blood bilirubin is more likely to cause damage to his brain than in a healthy baby.

Incidence of a particular type of congenital heart disease, *patent ductus arteriosus*, is higher in preterm babies.

He is more prone to develop *dehydration* and ankle swelling (*oedema*).

For various reasons, he is susceptible to develop many metabolic disturbances such as *hypoglycemia*, a condition in which blood sugar level is reduced.

He is prone to develop various nutritional deficiencies such as anaemia.

His resistance to infections is low.

Since liver and kidneys are not functioning adequately, he is more susceptible to the toxic effects of drugs.

The low-birth-weight baby sleeps nearly all through day and night. He lies without making much motion and cries very little.

Special care

Now that you have been told about the special problems of the low-birth-weight baby, it will be easy to understand that his needs are also special. His care is based on the principle of managing any newborn with certain modifications. Before we touch on those special features of care let us recapitulate the special needs of the low-birth-weight infant. First, his breathing must not only be established but also well maintained. Secondly, his body heat has got to be maintained. Thirdly, he must be adequately fed. Fourthly, he must be protected against infection. Lastly, any kind of physical tiredness should not be inflicted on him.

Now, it becomes easy to understand why such a baby should be born in a well-equipped Centre where good resuscitation facilities are available. It is customary for a senior obstetrician and a child specialist to be present in the labour room when such a delivery is anticipated. It is a practice to clamp the low-birth-weight baby's cord fairly late and to squeeze it to the baby's side before it is ligated. This gives the baby a good deal of extra iron stores.

Once the doctors are convinced that he is breathing properly and fluid and blood have been sucked out of his throat and mouth, he is immediately removed into a prewarmed *incubator* in which his body heat can be preserved, he can rest without external disturbance and also have a great deal of protection against infection. Most Centres nurse the incubator babies without clothes so that it is easy to notice development of jaundice, cyanosis etc.

He is left undisturbed. Visitors are not allowed. His mother may, however, be permitted to come and touch him. For this, she is trained to take strict aseptic precautions.

He is not given a bath until he is at least 2 kg in weight.

As for feeding, the details will be given in Section 11. As a rule, if he can suck well and swallow well, breast-feeding should be the choice. In others, the doctors may like to give feeds through a *nasogastric tube* or by *intravenous drip* if the baby is less than 1,200 gms in weight.

Also, remember, there is no sense in delaying the first feed. That can be dangerous. There is distinct advantage in giving the first feed as soon as the baby has recovered from the shock of "birth". It is rarely more than 2 to 6 hours.

Discharge from hospital and home care

Ideally speaking, a low-birth-weight baby should be discharged from the hospital when he has regained his weight, is able to feed satisfactorily, shows stable temperature control under normal room temperature and is free from disease. In our overcrowded hospitals and nurseries, it is usually difficult to fulfil the first criteria. Most babies are discharged when they reach 1,600 to 1,800 g in weight and show evidence of steady weight gain.

The mother should, however, make sure that she is fully trained to feed the baby, knows how to maintain aseptic environment around the baby and has learnt the ways and means to keep the baby warm.

At home, she must see to it that the handling of the baby by the visitors is discouraged.

If home visiting facilities by the doctor, lady health visitor or a public health nurse are available, she must make good use of these to assess the baby's progress as also for further advice.

Low-birth-weight baby and drugs

As I pointed out earlier, the low birth weight baby reacts poorly to most of the drugs. Your doctor, as you will notice, is likely to avoid medication to him unless it is urgently needed. He would skip administering drugs like chloramphenicol, sulphonamides and vitamin K to him. When he indeed prescribes, the dose is usually one half of that recommended for the normal newborn.

10

AFTER-DELIVERY CARE OF THE MOTHER

Well, you have had enough knowledge about the newborn. Isn't it time we relax for a while and talk a bit about you now?

So, listen.

Once the baby has arrived—hopefully healthy and without making you really sick—your body and organs will take another 6 to 18 weeks to return to "normal" and enable you once again to take up your old responsibilities plus the new ones. This period following delivery is known as *puerperium.*

How the body changes

A major change is the reduction in the size of the womb by a series of processes known as *involution.*

Imagine in 6 weeks time the weight of the womb reduces from 1,000gms to just 50gms. The size also comes down from $6 \times 4^1/_2 \times 3^1/_2$ inches to a mere 3x2x1 inches.

During the first week or two, a discharge comes out of the vagina. This is *lochia*. In the beginning (say for 3 or 4 days) it is dark red in colour as it is more or less pure blood. Later it becomes pale and then scanty and creamy. Take advice from an expert if it persists after 2 weeks, more so if there is reappearance of blood in it.

Remember, other reproductive organs also show involution but the speed is not as fast as in the case of the womb.

Following delivery, the temperature is usually a degree higher than normal. Do not worry; it will return to normal within a matter of hours.

The pulse behaves a little differently. It is almost always normal as you are over with the labour. In the subsequent week or so it is likely to slow down. Do not panic if it is just 50 or so per minute. That is normal.

In the first few days, you may pass a lot of urine. This is called physiological *diuresis* and need cause no anxiety. Likewise, urine examination may show a little of albumin. You may suffer from constipation too.

The changes in the breasts are remarkable. Initially they get congested followed on the third day by marked fullness and tenderness. Its initial secretion, as we have learnt elsewhere, is *colostrum*—a thick, sticky yellow fluid which is considered the ideal food for the baby at this stage. *True milk* comes a few days later. Initiation of milk production and the maintenance of lactation—remember it– depends a great deal on mechanical stimulation by sucking the nipple as also on your "will" to breast-feed the baby and make a success of it.

Mind you, the mother's body does not have absolutely foolproof involution of all the changes that it underwent during pregnancy and labour. The anatomical structure of the wall of the womb, for instance, is likely to remain permanently altered in some way or the other. Also, the vulva remains somewhat enlarged. The *striae* on the skin also are likely to remain as permanent scars.

Care during hospitalisation

Most Centres discharge the mother and the baby, if all is well, after 3 to 10 days. Going home as early as possible is now being increasingly encouraged.

In the hospital room, where you are shifted after the delivery, you are supposed to take plenty of bedrest, including sleep, for 2 or 3 days. Then you will be allowed to sit at the side of the bed. If you wish, you may have a warm bath which, in fact, you should.

In order to regain a normal figure, you must act on the doctor's advice to start exercises while you are on the bed. He may want you to begin these on the very first day or a couple of days later. Gradually, the range of exercises is increased. The *foot exercises* will help you not to suffer from pain and aches in the feet which is invariably encountered after resuming activity at home.

In the hospital, you must cooperate with the doctor and nurses who are regularly attending on you, taking care of medical problem, changing sanitary pads and making sure that superimposed infection does not occur.

As I said earlier, constipation is common in the beginning. A mild laxative usually works but, at times, the doctor may advise an *enema*, which means injection of soap and water into the rectum.

How about the episeotomy or perineal laceration stitches? If the material applied for the stitches is absorbable, these do not have to be removed. In others, removal of stitches is usually done after 7 days, before discharge from the hospital.

Most maternity centres would give you the chance to see your baby as soon as you are out of the shock of labour and are relaxed and comfortable. This may take a few hours. Do not be apprehensive in loving him, cuddling him and above all in developing a kindly relationship with him right away. You may put him to the breast as well. In all probability, he is going to stay in a cradle by your bedside—yes, right under your very nose.

And, do not neglect your diet. Take plenty of fluids and good nourishing diet if you want to regain your health and to successfully breast-feed your baby.

Care of the breasts is of utmost importance. Always keep a good, well-fitting brassiere on. Attend to the cleanliness of the breasts. Also, learn how to manually express milk out of them. You may have to do it at one or another time, especially when gross engorgement of the breasts becomes a problem. Learn from the doctors and the nurses things which will stand in good stead to you and the baby once you are back home.

Finally, some women who are greatly exhausted during delivery and are also nervous may develop emotional disturbances, irritability and apprehension after the birth of the baby. Depression and insomnia may worsen the mother's condition. The so-called *puerperal psychosis* responds well to reassurance and to drugs like tranquillisers and sedatives. If the condition takes a serious turn, the obstetrician would, as a rule, consult his psychiatrist colleague.

Care after returning home

Once you are back home, make use of the routine you learnt in the hospital and follow the doctor's advice and instructions religiously.

During the first week, take plenty of rest, a good deal of it in the bed. Have small strolls but do not exert too much. Climbing stairs is not permitted. If you do not get exhausted, you may render a helping hand to the mother-in-law or others in doing easy things. There is nothing wrong in doing light pleasant reading, listening to the radio or watching the television, the *idiot-box* as many would like to designate it. Also, do see the visitors but avoid longish chatting sessions.

After a week, you may increase your activity and render more help in cooking and other household affairs. You may now begin to climb the stairs. Sleep enough. Have a good nap in the afternoon too.

In the third week, you may go shopping to the nearby market. You may also go out for an evening walk. Expose yourself to fresh air in your lawn and to the sunshine.

Take care of your nutrition. Else you will be harming your physique as well as the baby you are breast-feeding. Include in your diet milk, cheese, eggs, fish, meat, fresh vegetables and fruits. Drink plenty of fluids; fruit juices are very useful.

It is quite possible your doctor has prescribed for you some haematinic tablets (iron, folic acid, vitamin B_{12}, B-complex or multivitamin in variable combinations) and/or calcium pills. See that you do not skip the dose.

What about bathing? As I said a little while ago, doctors do not usually forbid the "bath". In the very first 3 days after delivery, the mother is encouraged to go in for it. At home, you should have a daily bath (sponge in the first week and then shower), especially during summer days. But, if you are a very outgoing type and addicted to swimming, please avoid it at least for the first 6 weeks after delivery.

Buy yourself a nylon abdominal belt and use it constantly to safeguard against abdominal "paunch" and the waistline getting too big.

Something which always puzzles the young mother: When is "coitus" permitted after childbirth? Take an expert's good counsel. They say: "Avoid it during the first 6 weeks or so, perhaps a little longer if you can."

And, do not forget to continue the postnatal exercises that you learnt in the hospital. Make "exercise" a routine.

More about post-natal exercises

Household as an exercise: When you resume doing housework—do not delay it much—keep your posture straight and your muscles of the abdomen contracted. A lazy posture will make your muscles of the abdomen still more flabby and increase the waistline rather than make it trim.

Climbing stairs: Contract your abdominal muscles and then climb upstairs. Remember to walk two stairs at a time.

Standing exercises: Contract your abdominal muscles while you stand. Bend forward from the hips while you hold the back of a chair. Try to push the chair with the contracted muscles of the abdominal wall.

. Stand with contracted abdominal muscles against a wall. Try to flatten the middle of the back against the wall.

Lying-down exercises: There are quite a few of these.

To begin with, lie on back, hands behind the head. Now, slowly raise yourself to the sitting position.

Lie flat on back, arms stretched overhead. As you sit up bringing forward the body, try to touch the toes with your hands. Repeat several times.

Lie flat on back, feet crossed. Now make the muscles of the abdomen and seat tight by contraction.

There are many more.

Kneeling exercises: Begin by kneeling on all fours, keeping your head high. As you contract the abdominal muscles, tuck your head under the arched back.

As you keep your abdominal muscles contracted, kneel, sit on the heels and roll the head down on the knees.

11
INFANT FEEDING

So, once again back to the baby!

And, wait, the subject now happens to be as vital as *feeding*, without which the nutritional as also the emotional and psychological needs of the baby cannot be adequately met.

Milk, as you would understand, is the fundamental food for infant feeding, especially during the early months of life. Mother's milk is the baby's most natural food. It is also the best. We shall examine in the pages to follow why and how it is so.

This is not to say that artificial feeding with cow's milk or other breast milk substitutes has absolutely no place in infant nutrition. It has. There are situations warranting special diet for metabolic reasons, when mother's milk is not available or in view of some other pressing but genuine factor breast-feeding cannot be given. All these are indications for artificial feeding.

BREAST-FEEDING

Human milk has been hailed as "a unique gift of love and a natural resource" by Dr. Derrick B. Jelliffe, one of the greatest authorities in infant nutrition. Every baby, as far as possible, must be breast-fed at least for the first 3 months and preferably for the first 6 months of life. As and when there is doubt if the infant will be able to receive enough of proteins from elsewhere, he should continue to be fed on the breast for as long as 2 years or so. Remember, mother's milk is not a "poor babies' food" but food of choice for the infant.

Mother's milk is the best. Why?

You have full justification in asking why breast-feeding is considered the best. What are its outstanding advantages? It is as well that you should be aware of them. So, watch...

Tailor-made composition: Human milk has a composition that is ideally suited to meet the requirements of an infant. No other milk comes anywhere close to it in this connection. Remember, it may be possible to bring up an infant on milks of other species, it is quite impossible (at least not with the present technical knowhow) to humanise cow's milk or for that matter any other milk.

No preparation needed: Mother's milk is always fresh, pure and ready for instant use, requiring no preparation. Thus, exposure to external contamination is more or less avoided.

Adequately warm: Human milk is always at a temperature which is best suited to the infant. You do not have to boil it and then make sure that it gets to the right temperature.

Minimal contamination: Breast milk is more or less sterile. That it is safe for the baby is a remarkable merit *per se*. It has been convincingly shown in several studies that the incidence of respiratory infections such as cold and gastrointestinal infections like diarrhoea is much less in breast-fed babies. I have only infrequently encountered severe gastroenteritis in fully breast-fed babies though the disease is a leading cause of death and ill-health in late infancy. The experience of other workers is no different.

Anti-allergic property: Mother's milk contains antibodies against food proteins as also cow's milk proteins. Such antibodies are useful in blocking absorption of toxic or allergic food materials to which the infant has no local intestinal immune response of his own.

Many experts believe that breast milk, if adequate, should be the sole source of nutrition during the first 6 to 8 weeks of life. Introduction of foreign proteins, including cow's milk—remember it—very early in life only hastens and facilitates the induction of allergy.

Defence against infection: Just a while back I pointed out that mother's milk is safe and nearly free from contamination. All that reduces the chances of infection. But there is little more to the story.

It contains several anti-microbial factors (agents which resist the invasion) which play an important role in defence against infection in the baby.

There is also evidence of presence of antibodies against certain bacteria and viruses, and that includes virus that causes polimyelitis, the paralysing disease.

If you still need more evidence, listen to this. A recent investigation has demonstrated that the anti-infective factors continue to be present in significant amounts in mother's milk even at the end of the first year of lactation.

These qualities of breast milk are of major significance for the infant's defence against infection, particularly in the Third World countries where risk of infection is very high.

Economic significance: Decline in breast-feeding in Singapore during 1951-1960 led to a loss of 1.8 million US dollars.

On the world scale it has been estimated that marked decline in breast-feeding could lead to literally billions of dollars going down the drain.

Even if you do not care what happens to the rest of the world or the statistics, just wait. Does it cost anything to feed the baby on your own breasts? Imagine if you have to go in for all those bottles, teats and milk powders.

Healthy mother-child relationship: Yes, you guessed it well, breast-feeding contributes a great lot to establish sound and healthy mother-child interactions. The breast-fed infant has the close, warm contact of the mother's body that has been compared to the "warm encompassing amniotic fluid (the water in which the baby floats while in the womb) which he just left."

Nursing the baby would decidedly give you much satisfaction and a sense of fulfilment. The baby too gets reciprocal contentment and pleasure.

Contraceptive value: Breast -feeding, it is claimed, helps in spacing children. The chances of conception in a lactating mother are far less. Mind you, I said it "helps"—just helps, not that it is a dependable foolproof way for contraception.

Shaping mother's figure: There is no truth in the widely held belief that breast-feeding spoils the figure of the mother. Reality is just the other way round. Done properly, breast-feeding, in fact, improves and shapes the young mother's figure. It enables the uterus (the womb) to return to the normal size and also drains away extra fat that accumulates during pregnancy.

Protection against cancer: Mothers who breast-feed their babies show relatively a very low incidence of breast cancer. This is exemplified by the fact that breast cancer hardly hits the Jews who have a very high rate of breast-feeding.

Protection against degenerative disorders: In recent years, considerable evidence has accumulated to show that human milk offers some protection against arteriosclerosis, a degenerative disorder of blood vessels.

Contra-indication. Is there any?

If you are well and the baby is well there is absolutely no disadvantage and no contra-indication of breast-feeding. It is not only the superiormost type of infant feeding but also a "must" for the infant.

Think hundred times-with a cool mind—before opting against giving your own milk to the baby.

Mechanism of milk production

Your breast is composed of 20 odd lobes, also called segments. Placed more or less at the periphery are the secreting alveoli, surrounded by the cells of myoepithelium. The ducts from the alveoli converge to form a solitary duct of each segment, opening on the surface of the nipple.

During pregnancy, as you must have noticed, the breasts enlarge and the body prepares the ducts and alveoli for lactation.

After delivery, a hormone, *prolactin* (produced by the pituitary gland in the brain) begins to act on the alveolar cells and induces milk production. The activity of this hormone is, however, kept suppressed by the so-called *prolactin-inhibitory factor* which comes from the hypothalamus lying close to the pituitary gland. Sucking the nipple by the infant causes inhibition of this factor as also withdrawal of the two hormones, *oestrogen* and *progestrone*. Consequently the pituitary secretes a higher amount of *prolactin* which in turn enhances production of fat, proteins and lactose by the glandular tissue. Thus the milk secretion is initiated by prolactin. Its maintenance is regulated by the growth hormone and thyroxine, a hormone from the thyroid gland which is situated in the neck.

The propulsion of milk into the ducts and then from the nipple into the baby's mouth is again stimulated by sucking.

Sucking is, thus, of vital importance for both the phases of lactation. If the breast is not fully emptied, increasing pressure in the ducts is likely to inhibit secretions. The higher the demand, the greater is the production and supply of milk. That is why some women keep secreting enough milk years after the birth of their last child. There is a famous case of a wet nurse in the palace of Cadi of Biskra. She is said to have continued supplying lavish amount of milk 30 years after the last childbirth.

When does milk begin to come after delivery? It is on the second or third day in case of multipara. Primipara starts supplying milk a little later, i.e., on the third or fourth day. With the passage of days and weeks, the breasts tend to adjust well in their milk production to meet the infant's needs. This is one unique example of how efficiently nature works.

The milk secreted in the first few days is called. *colostrum* (witch's milk, as the cynics would have us believe but which is all nonsense). This is exceedingly rich in proteins and gets coagulated spontaneously on standing. Gradually, the protein content falls whereas the fat content shows a rise in colostrum as time passes. In the first month secretion of milk is called *intermediate* or *transitional* milk. Thereafter, it is the mature milk which supplies most of the required nutrients with the exception of iron, vitamins C and D and copper.

Promotion of breast-feeding

The following measures may be of value in promoting lactation and breast-feeding:

(i)   Adequate prenatal advice to the young mothers about the several merits of breast-feeding. As you have judged by now, proper reassurance and preparation for breast-feeding go a long way to make it a success as and when the baby comes.
(ii)   The breasts must be kept clean.
(iii) It should be periodically ascertained by your doctor that the nipples are neither retracted nor cracked or sore. Engorgement as also abscess interferes with successful lactation.
(iv)   The infant should be put to the breast as soon as possible after birth. This is usually workable within the first 3 hours.
(v)   All efforts should be made to keep yourself happy, confident and free from anxiety. Worry is the enemy of successful breast-feeding.
(vi)   There is nothing to beat the frequent sucking by the baby in promoting milk production. Your doctor will advise you if you need to take a drug to help you in producing more milk.
(vii) Do not forget to take good nourishing diet with plenty of water and fruit juices.

More about antenatal preparation for breast-feeding

As was pointed out in Section 4, the mother must start preparing fairly early in pregnancy to understand the different aspects of breast-feeding and tackle the various demands of the infant when he arrives. This is most desirable for successful breast-feeding.

Nutrition: If nutrition is poor, the mother's borderline malnutrition may become over. On the contrary, overeating may cause excessive gain in weight. Average gain during pregnancy in the first 20 weeks is 3 kg. A gain of 0.4 kg per week is considered safe.

Both malnutrition and overnutrition are risky for the mother as well as the baby. In both cases, successful breast-feeding is hindered.

Motivation: The expectant mother should learn mothercraft and attend to motivation for breast-feeding during discussion with the nurses, lady health visitors or doctors during pregnancy.

Attention to breasts: A careful examination of the breasts is indicated early in pregnancy. If the nipples are retracted (inverted) rather than protactile (everted), you should wear light-weight plastic shells under the brassiere.

Care should be taken to wash the nipples with plain tap water. Application of soap, antiseptic lotion or vitamin ointment is best avoided. During the last month or so, gentle application of plain *lanolin* cream is allowed. Scrubbing the nipples to make them tough is not in order and should not be resorted to.

Since it is usual for the breasts to increase considerably in size, particularly towards the last trimester, it is desirable to wear an uplift brassiere about one or two sizes larger. It helps to prevent sagging.

Prenatal expression of milk: It is debatable whether prenatal expression of colostrum should be practised.

Expressing the breast milk during the last weeks of pregnancy allows the mother to get used to the handling of her breasts by the future baby. Thus, she learns a technique that might prove handy once breast-feeding has begun.

Secondly, it is claimed that the more the mother expresses her colostrum, the more ready will the breasts be to produce larger amounts of milk after childbirth.

How to do manual expression? She should gently squeeze the skin above and below the nipple, avoiding the dark area with the forefinger and the thumb. This brings out a small amount of thick yellow material.

In the beginning the technique poses some difficulty. But, before long and with some practice, this becomes an easy thing to do. It becomes of great utility later when a few days after the birth of the baby her breasts get engorged. Unless she has initially expressed some milk, it becomes difficult for the baby to get his jaws around the nipple.

Techniques of breast-feeding: Every pregnant mother should learn during the antenatal period various skills like how to bear down, how to relax and how to promote lactation and how to actually breast-feed the baby.

She should also learn during this period how to do burping. Else, such little problems as "wind" discourage her from further feeding the infant on her breasts.

Feeding schedule

There is no hard and fast rule as to when to put the baby to breast after childbirth. In most cases it can be done within 3 hours and in nearly all by 6 to 12 hours. If you wish to do it immediately after birth, this will be ideal. The earlier you put him to breast, the greater are the chances of success in breast-feeding the baby. I am of the opinion that, soon after delivery, the baby should be left with the mother—all naked. Not only should he be encouraged to have skin-to-skin contact with her but he should also be put to the breast.

Unless the baby is premature, he does not need any supplement (not even water or just a little of the other milk) at this stage. He is born with enough of extra fluids which stand him in good stead until the mother begins to produce milk. Don't be panicky if the baby loses up to 10 per cent of his weight in the first week or so. This is all very normal. He should regain his birth weight by the 10th to 14th day, depending on the milk production by the mother.

Today, the superiority of the "demand schedule" over the "time schedule" is firmly established. You should feed the baby when the baby is hungry rather than when the clock gives the signal. Most babies over weeks become fairly regular in their feeding pattern. An approximately 3-hour schedule is the common pattern. Do learn to respond to the needs of the baby by feeding, rocking or changing the nappie besides, of course, giving him ample love.

The *adequacy of breast milk supply* is indicated by:

(i)   the baby sleeping 2 to 4 hours after the feed, and
(ii)   his gaining weight satisfactorily.

What is *test-feed*? You have perhaps heard about it and want to know more. Well, it involves weighing the infant before and after feeding him. The difference in weights indicates the amount of milk he has ingested. Nowadays, it is held that test-feed is not a very satisfactory way of assessing the adequacy of the milk supply. The method may also cause anxiety to the mother in case the intake is not as much as she wants. This may further reduce the milk supply.

The baby empties a breast in 10 to 15 minutes. Thus, there is no sense in keeping the infant on the breast for more than 20 minutes. Unless the quantity of milk is excessive, both breasts should be emptied at each feeding session.

Basic principles of breast-feeding

Firstly, the mother and the baby should be comfortable and relaxed at the nursing time. The mother, herself in a semi-recumbent position, should support the baby's buttocks on the palm of a hand and the head on her elbow. This is done in such a way that the face of the child is close to the breast which the mother supports with the other hand. This is important. Else, the baby may get choked.

I have spoken to a multitude of nursing mothers and they admit "this position helps" in successful breast-feeding. As a matter of fact, it is an observation that soreness of the nipple may occur as a result of poor attention to mother's and baby's positions during breast-feeding.

You should be well conversant with the technique of putting the baby to the breast and removing him from it. Learn it from a knowledgeable friend or a senior woman in the family or neighbourhood.

You shoud see to it that the baby empties at least one breast at each sitting. Of course, a little milk is likely to be left behind. Don't worry about it. If he is still hungry, offer him the other breast during the same sitting. At each sitting, the infant should start from a different side. So, mind you, the impression that only one breast must be given at each feed and that the second breast should be reserved for special situations is not well founded. Remember not to push the nipple into his mouth. There is no need to wash the nipple after each and every feed but it should, of course, be kept clean. Do not let your clothes rub and hurt the nipples. If you make it a point to support the breasts in between the feeds by a well-fitting brassiere, you will feel more comfortable and relaxed. Besides, this will also be helping to preserve your figure which, little wonder, is dear to you.

As was pointed out earlier, nursing time on each breast need not exceed 20 minutes. Do not keep the baby on the breast so long right from the very early days. Start with 5 minutes and then slowly increase the duration. Keeping the baby far too long will only make him fussy and take in wind rather than milk. All said and done, let it be clearly understood that the duration of a feed should be decided by the infant's hunger, by no means by the clock.

What is *burping*? It consists in holding the baby erect over the mother's shoulder or making him sit on the mother's lap and then patting or rubbing his back so that he eructates the swallowed air, the so-called *wind*. If you do not do so, you may well be allowing him to have regurgitation, vomiting and even abdominal colic. At times it may become advisable to bring the wind out half-way through feeding. There is nothing wrong with it.

A contented baby is a good guide as regards the adequacy of milk supply. The most reliable criterion of adequate supply of breast milk is the progressive weight gain. A baby who gains less than 500 gms in any 4 weeks in the first 3 months of life or 250 gms in the second 3 months is likely to be malnourished. Doctor's consultation needs to be sought. He will be able to evaluate as to what is wrong with the baby's intake. If there is any disease process contributing to the problem, he will look into it and guide you as to what to do.

And, do not neglect your diet, personal hygiene and health. Take sufficient rest. Do not indulge in using any drug unless prescribed by the doctor.

Caesarean section and breast-feeding

I am astonished at the increasing rate of failure to breast-feed. The increased incidence of Caesarean operation in the cities is adding to the "mess" since it is taken for granted by most obstetricians as also the folks that there is no question of breast-feeding after such an operation. The notion is simply absurd.

I do not find any convincing reason why a mother who has had this operation cannot breast-feed as successfully as the mother with normal vaginal delivery. Of course, because of the effect of general anaesthesia, you may take longer to start nursing the baby rather than immediately as is now recommended in normal deliveries. Also, you would have to put your discomfort and pain aside so that your baby is not deprived of the advantage of colostrum, the initial milk. In the beginning, since sitting may mean more pain, you are advised to nurse the baby while you lie on your side.

Some mothers are disappointed for having not experienced a normal childbirth. Breast-feeding should help to compensate for some of their disappointment.

So, even if you have had Caesarean section, do not allow the folks to discourage you from breast-feeding the infant. Your determination will make up for whatever negative points there may be, thereby making a success of this "gift of God".

Which mother, after all, would like to deprive her baby of the best food, her own milk?

Mother's illness and breast-feeding

In most instances, a mother can continue breast-feeding while she is unwell. In such cases, the doctors prescribe medicines that are less likely to harm the baby. In ailments such as septicaemia or jaundice, the doctors may discontinue breast-feeding for short periods. During this gap, the mother should express the milk to safeguard against breast engorgement and to ensure free flow of milk when she resumes breast-feeding after a few days.

As for the baby, feed him fresh milk with a clean spoon and cup during this passing phase.

Breast-feeding and drugs

Almost all drugs taken by lactating mothers are excreted through breast milk, usually in very small amounts. But, if a drug is required to be given in a large dose or over an extended period, breast-feeding may prove damaging to the infant. Antithyroid drugs given to the mother with thyrotoxicosis (a disease of the thyroid gland lying in the neck), for instance, may cause hypothyroidism in the infant.

An interesting topical issue is: What is the influence of the contraceptive "pill" on the breast-fed baby? The accumulated evidence suggests that certain types of pills (nearly all, remember it, contain hormones including oestrogen) do have an adverse effect on lactation. But, again a point that should not be overlooked is, that this is the case only when lactation is not yet established. The contraceptive pill does not, however, interfere with the fully-established lactation.

A question that should be tossing in your mind: is the consequences of the pill just a coincidence or indeed its pharmacological adverse effect? There is, in fact, as yet no right answer to it. It is very much possible that mothers who are in a hurry to start the pill are also the ones who unintentionally fail to encourage adequate sucking at the breast.

All said and done, it is advisable to wait for about 6 weeks before starting an oral contraceptive. In fact, as I put it at an earlier stage, it is advisable not to rush into coitus until at least 6 weeks have elapsed since the arrival of the child. By this time, lactation is fully established and will not be affected by the use of the pill.

Yet, if you must use the pill earlier, make sure that you go in for a preparation that contains low dose of hormones. In this case, remember to immediately give up the pill as soon as you feel your lactation has begun to be affected.

Baby's ailment and breast-feeding

Time and again, we continue to be asked: "Shall I stop breast-feeding him since he is not well?" The answer is a plain "No".

Your baby can and needs to be breast-fed even when he is unwell to provide him enough of nourishment and strength to fight the disease as also to recover from it. Antibodies in your milk will protect the baby from superadded infections which can attack a weak infant.

Only in rare instances, the doctors may want to put him off the breast temporarily. Here too, most frequently, the baby may be fed your expressed milk.

Breast-feeding and menstrual periods

"Doctor, I have restarted my periods. Is it safe to continue breast-feeding the baby?"—This and similar questions are invariably posed by the young mothers.

Well, in case your periods have returned (though it is not usual) while you are fully breast-feeding the baby, do not worry. Your milk will continue to be perfectly normal and suitable for the infant. Your anxiety may show up in the baby. Such mothers often complain that "the baby becomes somewhat irritable and fussy at the time of the periods."

So, go ahead with breast-feeding—periods or no periods.

Nursing mother's diet

In order to produce enough milk for adequate growth of the baby, you must eat a little extra of whatever you eat routinely. This is important to maintain your own health as well. A little additional helping of chapati or rice, green leafy vegetables, dal, fruits, egg, fish and meat should suffice. Overeating must, however, be avoided.

Many mothers hesitate to breast-feed their babies just because, as they put it, "I am so weak". Remember that even malnourished mothers are able to breast-feed their babies for the first 4 to 6 months. This, no doubt, puts extra strain on their vulnerable bodies, depriving them of calcium and proteins. The answer lies not in avoiding breast-feeding but in improving their own nutrition.

What "eats" the breast-feeding mother should avoid

Needless to say, you must avoid alcohol and smoking like the plague. I have spoken to numerous mothers who regretted terribly that they had smoked and, perhaps, drunk during pregnancy and after the birth of the baby. I have never come across a woman who has regretted having never indulged in any such thing.

It is well to remember that very spicy foods, such as chillies and flavoured foods, may cause a sort of smell in the milk that the baby finds annoying. These may also upset his tummy. As long as your baby is on your milk, you should avoid these.

Also avoid all such foods which are new to you and you are yet to be sure if these will suit you or the baby at all.

Bowel habit in breast-fed babies

Everyday I am fired with problems like "He passes very soft stools" by the mothers who are breast-feeding their infants. They wonder "If it is diarrhoea?" In fact, many of them admit having given several antidiarrhoeal drugs to the infants with no relief.

Well, soft and frequent motions are something which is normal for a breast-fed baby. It is surely not diarrhoea.

Yet, there are some breast-fed babies who pass motions just once in a day or two. Is it constipation? No.

In either case, there is no cause for worrying. Just keep your cool and continue to feed the infant on your breast.

Failure of lactation: reality or myth?

Many eminent researchers believe there is no such thing as failure of lactation. Says Dr. Derrick B. Jelliffe: "It is never real and is always avoidable."

Yet, there is no denying the fact that many women somehow do not really succeed in making a "go" of the breast-feeding. We have looked into this problem and feel that a good proportion of such mothers, in fact, have an indifferent attitude to breast-feeding. They regard it "messy", "an encroachment on their activities", "a silly thing to do" and so on and so forth. They have neither been motivated in the antenatal period nor encouraged after the childbirth to breast-feed the baby. If little effort has been put that is indeed very inadequate so that they are hardly conversant how to make a success of it.

There is a great deal of evidence that attitude of the mother has a great bearing on the success or failure of lactation.

Quoting Dr. Jelliffe once again: "One factor that proves disastrous as far as the success of breast-feeding is concerned is the availability of the feeding bottle around." So, one thing that you should never do is to rush for artificial feeding as soon as you encounter some difficulty in starting the baby on the breast. That will hamper the very production of milk by the mother.

Talking about the local conditions of the breast that may contribute to failure at the breast, let us first take up *sore* or *cracked nipples*. Leave the nipple dry rather than apply soap and water to it. Take the infant off that breast for a temporary period. Express milk from the breast and give it to the baby at the feeding time. Meanwhile apply lanolin or some cream as advised by the doctor to the nipple. In 2 to 3 days you will be able to resume breast-feeding.

Whether application of a nipple shield helps in any way is doubtful. One thing is sure: it makes it tough for the baby to get the milk supply once a shield is there.

Retracted nipples cause difficulty in the drawal of the areola into the baby's mouth, that is in sucking. Quite frequently, it helps to press the areola between the thumb and the index finger just before the nipple is put in the mouth of the infant.

If it does not work, you may use a nipple shield temporarily.

Eventually, you may have to resort to expressing the milk and give it with a spoon or a bottle.

Painful, grossly overdistended or *engorged breast* again needs expression of milk before baby is put to the breast.

So, mind you, just because you have some difficulty in initiating the baby on breast-feeding is not a good reason to "call it a day". Do not say that you have run out of luck. A positive attitude, determination and the "will to sort things out" can more often than not lead to success.

There are women who have failed to breast-feed in the past but wish to do it now. Dr. Ronald Illingworth's following advice to such mothers will, I believe, be of great advantage:

(i)   Ignore comments from your friends and relatives that you will not be able to feed your baby on the breast.

(ii)   Express the milk from the breast after every feed for the first 7 to 10 days, giving the milk by spoon if he will take it.

(iii) Let the baby feed when he wants to.

(iv)   Avoid giving a bottle feed at least for the first 4 days, unless on the fourth day there is virtually no available breast milk. He can be given boiled water, if the weather is hot, but cow's milk (fresh or dried) should be avoided unless it is absolutely essential.

(v)   Try to take adequate rest during the day.

(vi)   Do not conclude that your baby's crying or vomiting is due to insufficiency of milk unless, after a week, the weight gain is defective. Most babies should regain in birth weight about the tenth day.

ARTIFICIAL FEEDING

In spite of the widespread recognition that breast-feeding is the best for the infant, artificial feeding, especially in the form of bottle-feeding, has somehow come to stay.

What an expensive affair!

The mothers who opt for it as a matter of choice may take pride in saying it is simple, convenient and a sort of boon to their personal freedom. That it is expensive is hardly realised, not to speak of the several hazards it poses to the infant. An idea about the stress and strain that it can cause can be had from this example. Imagine a 4-month-old baby needing 2.5 kg of milk powder every month and even more as he grows a little older. Then there is all the equipment, including bottles and teats, which too cost something.

Artificial feeding may spell hazards

The lack of knowledge regarding proper feeding technique, poor socio-economic status, irrational beliefs, superstitions and customs, and preoccupation of the mother in other things figure prominently among the factors that make the bottle feeding hazardous to the baby.

Overdilution of the formula is the commonest problem which results in underfeeding and eventually in multiple nutritional deficiencies in the infant. Why do mothers overdilute the milk, be it mammal's or just the powder?

The reasons are multiple. In their own words "pure cow's or buffalo's milk is too concentrated for the baby." "Milk powders are too strong to be given as such", "Pure or low dilution milk causes tummy upset" and the like.

An unsaid cause is: mothers from the weaker section are keen to "ape" those from the elite. They must follow the fashion of employing the tinned milk powder, even though this—a luxury, so to say—can hardly be afforded by them.

The result: a highly diluted formula—apparently insufficient liquid feed—which contains very little solute and, thus, very little for adequate growth of the baby.

Superadded infections, especially acute gastroenteritis, as a result of dirt from poor hygiene and untidy hands as also feeding bottle and other utensils—a situation often encountered in the illiterate families—constitute another danger of bottle-feeding. Acute gastroenteritis may *per se* prove a "killer". In others, its recurrent attacks adversely affect the nutritional status of the baby, often leading to gross malnutrition in one shape or the other.

Iron and vitamin deficiencies, especially those of C and D, are common in artificially-fed infants unless they receive supplements of these constituents at the appropriate time.

Prolonged use of skimmed milk may cause vitamins A and D deficiency. Likewise, if a sweetened condensed milk is given for a long time, protein-energy malnutrition may result.

The choice is yours

Yet, if you feel you have got to give your baby artificial feeding, either on doctor's advice or on your own (I have a hunch that most often it will be the latter), the choice is yours. You must exercise greater vigilance and extra care in carrying it out. Do not forget to bear the following instructions if you do not wish to expose the baby to its hazards.

Which milk?

Cow's milk is preferred for artificial feeding especially if you do not want to make the things too expensive. Milk powders are costly but have the advantage of less contamination and adulteration. Buffalo's milk may also be used.

Cow's milk or modified buffalo's milk currently supplied by most State Government agencies (standard with 5 or 6 per cent fat; toned with 3 per cent fat, same as in cow's milk) form the basis of most of the formulae.

The recommended dilution for cow's milk for the first fortnight is 1:1. Subsequently it should slowly be decreased to 2:1, 3:1 and then given as such—yes, pure.

The suggested dilution in case of buffalo's milk remains more or less the same as with cow's milk.

Skimmed milk powder should not be used for infant feeding.

Not that there are no advocates of proprietary formulae. For instance, it has been suggested that large amounts of sodium consumed during infancy may cause high blood pressure in later life. If that be the case, feeding of proprietary formulae with low sodium content may be of advantage to the infant.

If you choose to give a powder milk, see that you start a standard brand and also make sure that its supply is not going to be short in the subsequent months. It is not advisable to keep changing the brand. If you have to do it because the particular brand does not suit your baby, do consult your doctor about it.

Remember to prepare the formula out of the powder milk as per instructions given on the tin or in a leaflet inside it. Generally speaking, one measureful of powder is to be added to one ounce of water. Do not ever overdilute the powder. You will get into a dangerous habit.

How much milk?

About 150 ml per kg per day is the average requirement for a healthy infant. Roughly, you should give one ounce per kg in each feed, not exceeding 8 ounces even by the end of the first year.

According to another formula which is applicable for the first 6 months only, the quantity of each milk feed in ounces=age in months +3.

The table below gives the average amount of milk needed for every feed. You will surely find it handy for reference.

Amount of Milk Per Feed

Age	Amount	
	Ounces	ml
First 2 weeks	2 to 3	60 to 90
Third week to		
2 months	4 to 5	120 to 150
2 to 3 months	5 to 6	150 to 180
3 to 4 months	6 to 7	180 to 210
5 to 12 months	6 to 7	210 to 240

Close on the heels of amount comes the number of feeds that should be given to the baby at different ages. You will find this information in the table below.

Average Number of Feeds Per 24 Hours

Age	Number
First 2 weeks	6 to 18
Second week to one month	6 to 8
1 to 3 months	5 to 6
3 to 7 months	4 to 5
4 to 9 months	3 to 4
8 to 12 months	3

You do not have to stick to the amount of milk in the feed and the number of feeds suggested here as guidelines very rigidly. There will be some variations from child to child.

Addition of sugar

Every 4 ounce of milk needs one teaspoonful of sugar. If the baby is constipated, the amount can be doubled. Brown sugar is to be preferred in constipated babies.

About feeding bottle and teats

Today the consensus is that it is better to feed with a spoon and a cup rather than with a bottle.

Talking about feeding bottles, there are quite a few brands in the market. A boat-shaped bottle with a teat at one end and a valve at the other is better than a soxhlet-shaped bottle, more so from the hygienic point of view. The second type is difficult to clean. The boat is, however, the widemouthed bottle.

As regards teats, those made of rubber and having bases are hygienically superior to the plain and finger-like ones. The hole should be made with a red-hot needle. It should allow 12 to 15 drops of milk every minute when the bottle is turned upside down. This enables the infant to take as much milk as he needs without getting choked. After the hole has been made, the teat should be sterilized. This assists in getting rid of the smell of the burnt rubber.

Hygienic preparation is a must

Preparation of the formula needs strict hygienic measures. Otherwise, the baby is highly prone to contract an infection from dirty hands, utensils, bottle, teats etc.

You should boil the bottle for at least 10 to 15 minutes in clean tap water. Do not boil the nipple/teats in the same container. Moreover, the latter should not be boiled for more than 3 to 5 minutes.

If you wish you may buy a chemical solution for disinfecting the feeding paraphernalia. Such a solution will stand you in good stead during journeys or at an outing.

Addition of vitamins and minerals

Your doctor will usually advise you to give the artificially-fed baby supplements of vitamin C (25 to 50 mg/per day), vitamin D (400 IU/per day) and iron (1 to 2 mg/day). All these may be available in a single preparation.

Babies addicted to the bottle

Every other day I see educated mothers with grown-up babies (not infrequently 2 or 3 years of age) clinging to the "feeding bottle", in my clinic. Asked if it does not look odd, the mother's reply is invariably round about this: "What can I do? He cannot do without it."

The fact remains that the mother has not whole-heartedly decided to wean him from the bottle or when she does so it is already too late.

You should begin weaning the child from the bottle as soon as he is 6 to 9 months of age. By the time he is a year old, there is no reason why he should still be using the bottle. The cup is the right thing for him. Do not let any bottle lie around. He would certainly create fuss for some days. Eventually he will learn to do without it. But, remember, it requires determination and not half-heartedness on your part.

Feeding the low-birth-weight baby

The low-birth-weight infant has an immature alimentary system which causes special feeding problems which need to be tackled in a special way.

You must appreciate that, in order to make up for his weight deficit, he needs more milk. He also needs additional vitamins, A, C, D, E and K, as also iron and folic acid about the first month.

As a rule, he should receive his first feed early rather than late. Most good centres have a policy to give the feed just 3 hours after birth.

If the baby is less than 1200 gms in weight, especially when breathing difficulty or abdominal distension are also present, doctors prefer to start intravenous drip in order to give 5 to 10 per cent glucose round the clock.

Most babies with weight over 1800 gms and some even with less of it are able to suck well from the breast or bottle. Doctors would like you to breast-feed such a baby. One precaution: feed the baby small amounts but make it at more frequent intervals.

Most babies weighing between 1200 and 1800 gms would need to be fed in the hospital through a tube passed through the mouth or the nose into the stomach. This kind of feeding is indicated if the baby becomes quickly tired or takes more than 20 minutes to finish the recommended amount of feed.

There are two types of tube feeding. First is the intermittent tube feeding in which milk is given at certain intervals. The other is the intragastric infusion in which a tube is permanently left in the stomach with the other end attached to an infusion bottle containing milk. Since the baby keeps receiving continuous supply of milk in this way, continuous intragastric milk infusion is now winning pride of place in feeding the low-birth-weight baby. With this regimen, the baby takes a higher amount of milk, weight gain is more, nursing time is cut and the baby is least handled. Moreover, chances of regurgitation and aspiration into the lungs are minimized. Hypoglycaemia (low blood glucose), a common complication in such babies, occurs only infrequently when the baby is fed by this method.

The doctors may ask you to supply your expressed milk for the baby. So, be prepared.

In order to express milk, cup the breast with your hand so that your fingers are behind the areola, the thumb is on top and the remaining fingers beneath. As you push the breast back towards the chest wall, squeeze the fingers rhythmically. Keep rotating your hand around the breast so that milk ducts in all directions get emptied.

Repeat the process in the other breast. Again return to the first breast. Do this changing back and forth several times.

Expressed milk should be collected in a previously boiled container. This milk (often separated into two layers which is all very well and normal) needs to be stored in a refrigerator before it is used. In case this facility is not available, you may store it in the coolest possible place in the house. In the latter situation, the milk must be used within 2 to 3 hours.

12

FEEDING PROBLEMS IN EARLY INFANCY

I have yet to see a mother who has not complained about one or the other feeding problem of the infant at some stage. Most of these problems are encountered in the newborn. What is remarkable is that almost all of these are preventable.

"Too little feed", "too heavy feed", "too frequent feed", "wrong feeding technique", "poor respect to hygiene" etc., rank prominently among the underlying factors.

Regurgitation

Several babies bring up a little of the feed along with swallowed air. *Posseting* is the name given to this condition.

With some babies posseting becomes a habit. They relish bringing back some milk and chew it just as a cow chews the cud. This is what is known as *rumination*. Though harmless, it does make the baby somewhat "smelly". In order that while doing so he does not inhale any bit of the regurgitated milk into the lungs, you should put him on his side. Never, never make the mistake of putting him on his back. If put on the side, it will also become difficult for him to regurgitate and to continue rumination.

You do not have to bother about regurgitation unless it seems to be interfering with the nutrition of the baby. Also, if the baby brings back the entire food, particularly more than once, you should seek the opinion of your doctor.

Many people say that regurgitation is because of the "wind production". Is the baby a small wind-producing machine? The fact is that the wind in his stomach is the result of the excessive air that he swallows with the feed or because of excessive crying.

If you are well trained in the technique of *burping* and if you are putting it into practice, the solution of the problem is round the corner. In fact the problem should not occur if you are doing good *burping*. You may well check up with your doctor how to do it properly.

Vomiting

It may be due to overfeeding, prolonged burping, too much of swallowed air, gastroenteritis or some other infection.

Persistent vomiting is an indication for looking up the doctor.

Also, if the baby shoots the milk half-way across the room, you must consult the doctor. The so-called *projectile vomiting* may well be a manifestation of hypertrophic pyloric stenosis, a disease needing specialised care and in all probability an operation.

Sucking and swallowing difficulties

Remember, some difficulty in sucking during the first few days after birth is normal. This is the time when you and the baby are still trying to master the technique.

Certain mechanical problems, such as cleft palate, cleft lip, very large tongue, and obstruction in the nose, may interfere with feeding. Local conditions of the breast like sore and cracked nipples, retracted nipples and engorgement also cause sucking difficulties as was discussed in the last section.

Mind you, a preterm baby has greater chances of having poor sucking and swallowing difficulty.

If your newborn has developed jaundice (yellow discolouration of the skin and white of the eye) has poor activity and has stopped sucking well, do not delay reporting to the doctor.

Dehydration fever

Disinclination to feed, fever and drowsiness may occur in some newborn babies about the third or fourth day of life. Though you do not have to panic about this association of manifestations, its persistence is a case for seeking medical advice. The doctor may like to rule out urinary tract or any other infection. Most child specialists, even if a specific site of infection is not detected, like to prescribe antibiotic cover to such a baby, particularly if he is immature or is at a special risk because of one or the other reason. The very suspicion of a fulminant infection is considered an indication for such a treatment.

Dehydration fever usually comes down following addition of extra water for about 12 hours to his intake.

Excessive crying

Crying in a newborn is almost always a manifestation of hunger or thirst, chilliness, need for the mother's handling, or a wet nappie.

Repeated crying may begin to get on the mother's nerves. An insecure mother may fail to develop the much-needed warm emotional relationship with such a baby. The mother may indulge in battering. It is not uncommon to hear comments such as "What else can you do with such a rascal? He does not let me relax for a minute."

The subject of excessive crying is discussed at length elsewhere.

Colic

Sometimes a baby begins crying soon after birth and keeps doing so, particularly towards the evening, during the first 3 months or so. This condition has been christened *three months colic*.

Excessive intestinal mobility (activity) is said to be the cause.

You may consult the doctor who would reassure you and, perhaps, prescribe a mild antispasmodic agent.

Change in bowel habit

Infants on cow's milk, especially if underfed and given inadequate fluids, may pass constipated stools (the stools which are hard in consistency), causing a good deal of straining and discomfort. As a result, the fear of pain may further aggravate the condition. Retention may occur. Passage of such a stool on its own or following rectal examination may lead to anal crack or fissure. Some babies may have spurious diarrhoea.

You should give such a baby plenty of water, some brown sugar, honey or glucose.

If constipation persists, medical opinion should be sought. Cretinism (deficiency of thyroid hormone) and congenital megacolon (constriction of the distal portion of the large intestine) need to be ruled out.

Recurrent episodes of loose motions are often due to poor bottle hygiene. If you are fully satisfied there is no such problem, ask for doctor's advice. The baby may be allergic to milk or may be suffering from cystic fibrosis—a hereditary disease of the pancreas, the so-called sweet-bread, which is situated in the abdomen and plays an important role in digestion.

Underfeeding

A highly diluted formula, often due to ignorance or economic considerations, is a well-known cause of failure to gain weight. Such a baby is underfed and takes his food quickly showing that he has been hungry for long. Dissatisfied with the amount made available to him, he usually cries and cries until he goes to sleep. After a few hours, usually much before the due time for feed, he wakes up and cries.

Do not let such a thing happen. It is a sign of *bad mothering*.

Overfeeding

It is not a common problem in our country. Most infants, as a rule, refuse to accept excess feed. And pushing the feed forcibly is quite a difficult job.

But, then, some mothers do manage to give the baby larger feeds. These babies are likely to suffer from the so-called *infantile obesity*. In our experience, in this country too, incidence of infantile obesity is on the increase, especially in well-to-do families.

Mind you, pushing the feed more than the baby's needs does not always cause obesity. Some infants just stop gaining weight. Such a baby is unhappy, vomits large amounts of feed, has fatty diarrhoea and keeps crying.

Just think over: Who is responsible for the sorry state? The baby? You? Or God?

Inadequate mothering

Not all mothers are good enough and well prepared for the newborn. Some are sadly wanting in self-confidence and unsure as to how to handle the baby.

They are not well-versed in what is called *mother-craft*. They worry too much and are very apprehensive. Their nervousness somehow influences the baby. As a result, he becomes more demanding and cries a lot to the mother's further annoyance.

This interaction may lead to a rather unhealthy relationship between the mother and the baby. Eventually, his feeding suffers considerably and he fails to thrive.

13
INTRODUCTION OF SEMI-SOLIDS AND SOLIDS

Now that you have made a head start with the feeding of your baby, remember too that "milk", though an excellent food, is just not everything in infant nutrition.

Milk will serve well during the first 3 to 4 months of life. If you continue depending on it as the only food for the baby in the subsequent months too, I am quite positive you would have to cut a sorry figure. Repent. Repent. Yes, "repent"—that is what I said. Your baby's health and nutrition will begin to suffer because the intake of only milk fails to meet the infant's increasing demands of calories. For once, he will gradually become anaemic since milk does not supply enough iron to meet his needs and by this time his iron stores (with which he was born) are also depleted. This is what is known as the *milk anaemia*, a sort of postscript to the baby's erratic feeding.

Another reason for starting semi-solids at 3 to 4 months age is to provide the infant a chance for discovering varying tastes of different foods. Remember that taste buds begin developing at this period of life.

Three to four months period is the best time to begin learning the act of chewing and, in the process, strengthening the gums.

What to do? When to do it?

Do not let the solution get out of hand. Your baby needs semi-solids and solids in addition to milk after a certain age. You must remember to introduce the first such supplementary food when he is 3 or 4 months old. This is the time when his taste buds have just developed or are in the process of developing. It will be easy to get him used to foods other than milk right away. If you make the mistake of delaying the introduction of such foods, he is likely to create fuss in accepting these later.

What a pity that though introduction of semi-solids and solids has a high place in our country, it is carried out fairly late in most communities! It is celebrated as a ritual, the so-called *Annaprasana*, in most parts of India. Usually the family priest is consulted for an auspicious time, day and date. The ceremony seldom happens before the child is 6 months of age. On an average, *Annaprasana* is celebrated at the age of 9 months for males and 10 to 12 months for females. Too late! Too late!

It is up to you to stick to a ritual which is not in the interest of your child or to pay heed to scientific reasoning. If you care, you will be able to convince the elders in the family—if that at all is your problem—about the rationale of early introduction of semi-solids and solids in the baby's feeding regimen.

What is weaning?

Before I take up little details about what semi-solids and solids to give, when to give and how to give to the infant, just a little clarification about the term *weaning*. You surely have heard it often or read about it in different contexts.

The dictionary meaning of the term is "to be taken off the breasts", "to accustom to food other than mother's milk", "to coax away from..." or "introduction of top feeding". So much of confusion, you see. But do not bother. When we talk about infant feeding and use the term "weaning", what we usually mean is introduction of solids and semi-solids. It is as simple as that.

Adding new food: what, when, how?

Anything that is easily digestible can be introduced. Begin with one food at a time. Watch how the child reacts to it. Wait for a week or two before you introduce another food. Give the food in small amounts and slowly increase the quantity as he begins to like it and to tolerate it satisfactorily. Do not force the food and do not give it when you are in haste or in a bad mood.

You would like to know whether to give it before, after or half-way through his milk feed. You may use your good sense and your knowledge about the personality and behaviour of the infant in deciding this. It will vary from baby to baby but what is important is that this variation is perfectly within normal limits.

Also, it is my observation that some do not like to at once take to the spoon but they settle with it in due course. At times, the baby may spit every time you give a particular food. Withdraw it and try after a week or so. He may accept it. Yet, some babies are a little different. They begin to take a certain food but after sometime reject it.

So, let us see, how you should proceed with the introduction of new foods.

You should start with a fruit or a cereal when your baby enters his fourth month.

If you choose a fruit, I would suggest that you better begin with a mashed ripe banana. Its nutritional value is good, its availability is no problem and most babies like it and love to take it. You may give a teaspoonful of it—yes, mashed with hygienic precautions—as such or mixed in a little milk. Slowly, increase the quantity. Before too long, to your surprise, he will be eating one full banana.

In my experience, a considerable proportion of babies who do not relish bananas, do take favourably to a pure concentrated banana food available in the market as *Banalona*. It provides 87 per cent of carbohydrates plus proteins and minerals. It is easy to prepare. Do read instructions in the leaflet provided inside its tin.

You may give other fruits such as apple, chiku, mango, papaya (papita) and the like may also be given. Do not forget to mash these too.

If you are beginning with a cereal, or perhaps you can introduce it a week or so after the mashed fruit, *suji* (semolina) occupies the pride of place. Make a paste of the roasted suji, sugar and milk. On the first day, give just half to one teaspoonful but gradually increase the quantity to about half a cup.

You may give any other cereal. In fact, there is not much to choose between them. A rice and pulse mixed preparation, *khichri*, is popular in north India in particular. Powdered rice when cooked in milk also makes an excellent custard for the infant.

The market is flooded with precooked cereal preparations, such as *Nestum, Cerelac*, or *Farex*. These require to be prepared as per instructions printed on the tin. These foods are based on a mixture of powder milk with some carbohydrates like rice and wheat, and are, undoubtedly expensive. A wise energetic mother should, rather than spending large amounts on these tinned baby foods, provide her growing infant with all the nourishment that he needs from the very foods she employs to make the family meals. Moreover, the foods prepared at home are fresh and give the infant a chance to taste "variety".

A couple of months after the introduction of fruit or cereal, start boiled and mashed vegetables (as such or mixed in a little milk). Tomato is strongly recommended. You may give any seasonal vegetable, say green leafy vegetables, carrots, beans, peas, etc. Avoid, however, radish, onion, and turnip.

Once the baby has crossed 6 months of age, you may give him fish, egg, meat and other animal proteins. The late addition of these foods is to avoid the possible risk of allergy to the foreign proteins. Egg is very good. Begin with its "yolk". The "white" may be given some days or weeks later. Never give a raw egg.

By the time the baby is nearly 9 months old, he is taking 4 or 5 semi-solids or solids. His milk intake is much less now. Do not panic about it. It is all natural. Stop mashing the foods now. Try to give him biscuits, curd, bread etc. In fact, he has cut some teeth and should begin to take the family food. Encourage him if he attempts to eat by himself as a part of his growing and learning.

The whole process of weaning should be gradual and completed by the time the child is between 9 months and one year. Thereafter, he should be taking almost the adult diet of about 1,000 calories daily. By this time, he should be taking just two servings of milk, a total quantity of half a kilo or so. If you insist on too much of milk, he will not take enough of other foods. There will be no point in grumbling then and boring the doctor that "the baby eats almost nothing" although you keep running after him with it.

Remember, even a one-year-old may need softening of hard foodstuffs and exclusion of spices. Just two or three feeds a day will not suffice for him. He needs to be fed more frequently—every 2 to 4 hours which means about 5 times a day.

An often-asked query is: When should the infant be given semi-solids etc, before or after a breast-feed? You should give the baby such a food a couple of hours after a breast-feed when he is likely to evince greater interest in it.

Should soft foods be discontinued when the baby is sick? No, not at all. On the other hand, his needs for nourishment during illness are enhanced. Because of poor appetite, he may like to take foods other than what he normally eats. During convalescence, as his appetite improves, you should further boost his intake so that he regains his health fast.

Before it slips my mind, let me tell you that, along with the introduction of semi-solids and solids to the baby, you should begin to give him water as well. During hot summer months, introduction of water may be done rather earlier. Make sure that the water you give is boiled for about 10 minutes and then cooled. Avoid using a feeding bottle for this purpose. Instead, feed with a spoon to begin with and with a cup or a glass when he is about 7 or 8 months of age.

Finally, a word about the water and food hygiene. A little relaxation on this front can cause many a problem in the form of infections—the leading one being gastroenteritis which is known to account for a big chunk of infant morbidity and mortality. Let me summarise the precautions you must take:

1. Ensure a clean environment and home surroundings;
2. Strain drinking water through a clean cloth, boil for about 10 minutes, allow to cool and store it in a clean well-covered container, or use only filtered water;
3. Wash the utensils well and rinse them under running water before use;
4. Wash your hands with soap and water before you cook the meal, prepare the feed or feed the baby;
5. Avoid giving the baby a food that is kept overnight since such a food stands good chances of getting infected.

So, remember, diarrhoea in the baby is due to neither introduction of soft foods nor teething as is generally believed. It is due to contamination of water or food that the baby takes. It may also be due to the baby's tendency to pick up contaminated objects lying around and chewing them when he is teething.

14

INFANT-PARENT LOVE BONDING

One Monday morning, a young lady entered my hospital clinic, saying: "Sometime back I read your article in *The Times of India* highlighting the role of 'love' in achieving speedy recovery in little babies suffering from various ailments. Do you really mean it?"

Warm relationship

Well, well, I maintain that the infant's experiences of tender, loving care he receives can make a sick baby well as its lack can make a healthy baby sick. These are not only of immediate consequence but may also have far-reaching effects. These can, for instance, affect his future ability to love and develop deep and enduring relationship as also positive achievements. As Helene Arnstein puts it, "parenting with the hopes of raising children to become loving, warm and living humans can make this world a better one for all of us." Hate decidedly—yes, decidedly-narrows as love expands.

Let me take off by narrating this interesting ancient story:

A holy Roman emperor, Frederick II, who lived in the thirteenth century was eager to discover in what language orphaned children would first speak if no one talked to them beforehand. Would it be Hebrew, Greek, Latin, or Arabic? Or would it be the language of their natural mother? The emperor then brought together a group of these orphaned infants and told their foster mothers and nurses to suckle them, to keep them clean, but not to prattle or murmur to them, and certainly not to speak to them. Unfortunately, the emperor could never find the answer to his questions, because the babies all died. For, as the chronicler of those times, Salimbene, wrote, "they could not live without the petting and joyful faces and loving words of their foster mothers."

Another study, again quoted here, courtesy *The Roots of Love* by Helene Arnstein, dealt with children living in various kinds of institutions under varying circumstances and degrees of deprivation in late 1940s. In one founding home housing 91 infants, the babies had been fed breast milk by their mothers during the first 3 months of life or by foster mothers if the biological mothers were not available. Then they were separated from the mothers but still properly fed and kept clean and given good medical care. However, they were given no personal handling or affection—no petting, no joyful faces and no loving words. What they really got was one-tenth of the normal emotional supplies provided in the usual mother-child relationship. Result: stark emotional deprivation. Within 3 months, they became depressed and just lay passive and listless in their cribs. Lack of fondling and stimulation made their facial expressions empty, often imbecile. Rapid deterioration set in with regard to their mental status. By the end of the second year, the intelligence quotient (IQ) was found to be as low as 45, the "idiot" level. They gave no response whatsoever to the face or figure of anyone who approached them. With a few exceptions, they could not sit, stand, walk or talk. Many of the children simply wasted away and died.

Moral: Love is essential for survival and healthy growth of the child. The infant-parent love reaches out to and is felt by many families. A relationship that sheds warmth, friendliness and openness is, as Sigmond Freud puts it, "a joy for over and for all."

The crucial early contacts

Don't walk off with the idea that the love needs of the child begin only once he is somewhat grown up. Far from that. The fact is that in the very first minutes and hours after birth, intensity of intimate contact between the newborn on one hand and the mother and father on the other hand considerably influences the growth, development and attitudes of the child as also the parents' love bonding to him. When he is brought close to the mother's body and held gently and affectionately in her arms, he, of course, quietens down. But more than that this act switches on a unique sort of "communication" between the two. The reassuring arms of the mother provide an alternative to the security of his former life in the warmth of the womb where he was being continuously lulled by the regular sounds of his mother's heartbeats, by her rhythmic breathing and gentle, rocking movements of her body. Most authorities, including Marshal Klaus, believe these early moments in the baby's life are the ones when the father should also sit or stand beside the infant and the mother and actively participate in the "communication" for healthy future bonding.

The newborn's handiest reflex response is his extraordinary readiness to "root", meaning that when you touch his cheek or lip with the nipple he turns his head towards that particular side and attempts to find the nipple. Once he has found it, he naturally embarks on his most vital asset—"sucking". It is now universally agreed that breast-feeding is undoubtedly the most powerful way to forge a loving bond between the child and the mother.

Mary MacDermot and her associate researchers from Perth, Australia, have now convincingly demonstrated that the newborn is capable of seeing and forming impressions of what he observes in the environment as early as the first few days of life. In a recently-released volume, *The Remarkable Newborn*, they comment: "You try placing a bright object or light before his eyes and then move it around. Watch, he will follow it within the range of his vision." Let me make it clear to you that though the newborn does "see", he is not yet ready to understand what he sees.

The newborn is, of course, not quite sensitive to distant sounds such as thunder in the sky, traffic noise in the street, noises in the adjoining room, or barking of the dog in the neighbourhood. But he is definitely responsive to human voices, such as his mother's or father's, close to him. As Marshal Klaus stresses, "there is much sense in the mother or father's indulging in some kind of talk with the infant very early in life, and that too fairly frequently, not once in a blue moon, for developing healthy relationship."

While we are still on the "sound", let me remind you (of course, here's hoping you have already heard of it) that mothers everywhere hold their little bables in their left arms. Why? The baby can actually hear and feel the heartbeat. The rhythm gives him comfort, often putting him to a hearty nap.

Changing attitudes of the infant

Many mothers get upset that their first ploys with the baby are more or less one-sided affair where they give and give, attending to his endless demands and needs, and get very little in return. Admittedly, there is a lot of truth in this observation. Most often the only clearly perceptible way in which the baby manifests that he appreciates his mother coming to his help is by stopping crying. He is virtually a self-centred egoist though he is not at all aware of what "ego" is. His whole being aims at a search for release of tension of need (hunger). But, mind you, this is a passing phase and soon—very soon indeed—you will find that the infant begins to return your love in more than one ways. He will no longer be wrapped up in himself, using you as a sheer need-fulfilling object for his benefit.

By the time the infant is about a month old, he has somewhat come out of his shell. He makes his pleasure quite evident when picked up, fondled, caressed or talked to by slowing down his breathing, opening and closing the mouth and bobbing the head backward and forward.

According to the famous child psychoanalysis, Professor Selma Frailberg, during the first six months the baby has rudiments of a love language—the language of smile, the language of vocal sound-making, the language of embrace etc. "It's the essential vocabulary of love before we can yet speak of love... when the baby is grown up and 'falls in love' for the first time, he will woo his partner through the language of the smile, through the utterances of endearments and the joy of the embrace." His smile, in a way, is to show you his gratitudes for responding so readily to his needs. Remember, if during the first 5 or 6 months the baby throws smiles to others as well, he does so because he is yet to be able to distinguish his parents from all the other people in his environment. It is by about the sixth month (or perhaps a month sooner or later) that he really begins to show his particular preference for the mother or father. This indeed is the beginning of actual expression of love by the infant.

All too soon, as the baby enters the second six months of life, the fact that he wants his mother-or mothering person—around him, near him, with him and for him day in and day out becomes immensely clear. As one mother puts it, "the amiable socialite who only till recently accepted and enjoyed the company of family folks begins to cling to the mother." He simply but surely rejects others, often leading to a scene embarrassing to the mother as well as others.

This phase requires special tackling, teaching the baby how to love the mother as also others such as father, brothers, sisters, uncles, aunts, and grandparents and, at a little later stage, those outside the close family circle.

At the age of 8 to 12 months, the infant demonstrates an inclination for companionship with other children. Many a parent begins to worry "why the baby is going away from us so early in life."

Recapitulating from my earlier article on adolescence which appeared in *Women's Era* in 1984, let me remind you, dear readers, that such a tendency occurs at puberty too with loyalty to the gang and a strong sense of dependence and comradeship. In later adolescence, it takes the form of devotion to a hero, a beloved or a cause.

You must remember that all this is a transient physiological phase. If you let your hair down rather than show unnecessary anxiety over it, the child will grow out of it "rather mentally and socially healthier" as says J. A. Hadfield in *Childhood & Adolescence*.

Loving does not cause overdependence

Over the years, I have seen that some infants, particularly towards the tail-end of first year, are overdependent. They are the ones who stand a very high chance of becoming oversuggestible later. I have often been told, usually by the grandparents or other relatives, that this is the result of overindulgence, overprotection and overpetting by the mother, the father, or both. As one granny said, "he has had every-wee-bit done for him so that he can do virtually nothing for himself—not even go out for a toy."

I do not deny this can be the case in some selected cases, more so if the infant is already of a dependent temperament. But, mind you, the incidence of such overdependence is not much.

I believe that the most common cause of abnormal dependence is not being loved or cuddled too much. It is just the opposite. That is to say, lack of satisfaction of the need of dependence.

So, let no mistake be made, a child of around one year needs to be given a good deal of a sense of protection. Avoid all kinds of fears and shocks. As and when he falls sick, give him all sorts of comforts and assurances. A disturbing experience without reassurance is likely to cause a feeling of insecurity that may persist all through life.

Second year "trio"

In the second year of life, the child (who was in the first year all dependent on the mother) goes out to meet the world in self-display, curiosity and exploration. He wants to do everything in imitation. So, for Heaven's sake, don't be shocked at his not leaving you a moment's peace.

The trio of self-display, curiosity and exploration is very natural. The child should have an opportunity to demonstrate it in an atmosphere of love and security. How else will he gain a good deal of knowledge and experience before launching out in the ups and downs of life?

Imagine a child being denied outlets for one or all the components of this trio, by being constantly scolded for one or another. Result: he becomes bored and inhibited. He may restart clinging to his mother's apron and may even develop thumb-sucking or some other behaviour problem.

"Self-will": Do not crush it

In contrast to the phases of dependence in the first year and exploration in the second year, a child of around 2 years, having already explored about the world, is now all set to exercise his "will" and make the parents conform to his will. Freud rightly calls the age of two the age of "self-will".

He must give expression to whatever impulse is aroused in him. He must have his own way. If he wants to go out, he hates being stopped. If he wants lollypops, he insists on having them. If you say "no", he is bound to throw tantrums.

I know of a mother who reacted to such tantrums of her 2-year-old in these words: "O, hell, is beginning to get on our nerves, imposing his stupid 'will' on us season in and season out. We cannot allow him to grow like that. Can we?"

As you can see, this mother (perhaps the father too) set out on a mission—yes, to break the little toddler's will. Did they succeed? Of course, they did—well, obviously by an appeal to fear, punishment and threat. But at what cost? In their eagerness to make the child good and refined, what they got was a toddler who was docile, lacking in initiative and sense of will. What a pity, that by crushing his assertiveness, the mother robbed him of the strength of character and caused bottlenecks in his ability to adapt to life and overcome the ups and downs of life!

My objective in mentioning the above case study is to bring home to you the fact that crushing a 2-year-old's "will" and "self-will", often to the extent of aggressiveness, may lead to far-reaching adverse consequences.

First, it may (in fact, it is more often than not) result in sullenness and resentment.

Secondly, it makes the child sapless, spineless and unable to meet responsibilities or take initiatives, though apparently he becomes a good boy.

Thirdly, the child falls into a state of insecurity, anxiety and apprehension.

Fourthly, as a means of getting his own way, he may develop neurosis.

The way out

You may well ask: "Well, Doc, what then should the parents do about the self-willed child who makes everybody's life miserable?"

Of course, the answer is (what else ?) to make all efforts to find the right outlet for his "will" or "self-will", whatever it is. If he wants to do something naughty, why not teach him how to do it? A child who is not repressed and is allowed to do things (of course, somewhat "guarded") learns how to do them well. On the other hand, it is the repressed, frustrated one who is likely to get into trouble.

Finally, let me repeat what I wrote some years ago in *Women's Era*: Let the love bonds between the child and the parents grow rather than come under strain.

15

WATCHING THE BABY GROW UP AND DEVELOP

Watching your baby grow in size and unfold the various stages of development such as to reach for your hand, to sit, to walk and to speak is undoubtedly one of the most fascinating pursuits. The experience gives you lots of enjoyment, pleasure and, what is more, knowledge and understanding of the child. And, understanding of growth and development, mind you, contributes enormously to the child's intelligent management.

One suggestion that will stand you in good stead and give you immense satisfaction and pleasure once the baby has rapidly grown up: Maintain a *baby booklet* and jot down the points of interest about your observations in the child's progress.

What is growth and development?

Growth is a measure of physical maturation. It signifies an increase in the size of the body and its different organs. Thus, it can be measured in terms of centimetres or inches and kilograms or pounds.

Development is a measure of functional maturation. It signifies accomplishment of mental (acquisition of skills etc.,), emotional (development of attitudes etc.) and social (adaptability to family and society etc.) abilities. Unlike growth, it is rather difficult to assess development.

You will appreciate that, generally speaking, growth and development are so closely interrelated that it is virtually not quite possible to separate one from the other. Consequently, in practice, the two terms are either used together or, if used separately, usually denote synonymous meaning.

Growth of different body systems is at a different pace. The nervous system shows maximum growth in the first year of life. Thereafter, it grows very little. A serious disturbance of growth may affect the development of brain. As a result, delay in the acquisition of such skills as walking, social adaptation and speech.

It must be clearly understood that the speed at which growth occurs is not the same at various age periods. In the first 6 months it is exceedingly rapid so that a 6-month-old is double his birth weight. By the end of the first year, the birth weight trebles. A child of 2 years weighs four times his birth weight. In the following years and until puberty, growth remains at a lower pace.

It is of interest to note that at different ages, the body growth is not uniform. As for instance, during infancy, the head is much larger in relation to the size of the rest of the body. This proportion gradually changes to assume the adult ratio in the subsequent years of childhood and during adolescence.

Also, in younger children, the limits are relatively short. With the passage of years, their length increases at a greater pace than that of the trunk and the head. Doctors find the relationship between sitting height (trunk and head) with total height a useful index in the diagnosis of certain disorders of growth.

Types of body build

Ectomorphic build refers to relative preponderance of linearity, light bone structure, small musculature and subcutaneous tissue in respect to body length and large surface area.

Endomorphic build refers to a relatively stocky structure and a large amount of subcutaneous tissue.

Mesomorphic build falls in between the above-mentioned builds. Here the individual has relative preponderance of muscle, bone and connective tissue with a heavy, hard physique of rectangular outline.

What influences growth and development?

Not one thing but quite a few factors.

In the first place, *hereditary factors* have a great bearing on the eventual constitution of the body. Tall parents are very likely to have tall children.

Nutritional factors also influence the growth and development in a considerable way. Malnutrition retards a child's physical growth and development. There is some evidence that it may affect his intellectual performance if it occurs fairly early in infancy and still worse if it affects the baby in the womb.

Several other factors, including socio-economic status, emotional, environmental and seasonal influences, chronic diseases and infections also affect growth.

How far the growth potential influences growth has been a somewhat controversial issue. However, it is generally held that the smaller the child at birth, the smaller is he likely to be in the subsequent years. The bigger the child at birth, the bigger is he likely to be later. Thus, the growth potential is somewhat indicated by the child's size at birth.

Weight

On an everage, the ideal birth weight is said to be about 3.4 kg. The infant doubles his weight by the age of 5 to 6 months and trebles it by 1 year. He increases it 4 times in 2 years, 5 times in 3 years, 6 times in 5 years and 10 times in 10 years.

You must have your child weighed at birth. He should also be frequently weighed in the first few weeks of life. A poor weight gain may be a warning signal drawing attention to a disease or underfeeding. Do not weigh him every now and then after that. The practice is not only unnecessary but also undesirable. You will only be wasting time by doing so and also inviting unnecessary worries.

I would suggest the following schedule for weighing the baby:

First—at birth
Second—at one week
Then every week till he is 3 months of age
3 months to 6 months—every fortnight
6 months to one year—every month
1 to 2 years—every 3 months
Thereafter—every 6 months

As long as your child is happy, energetic and kicking about and the doctor feels he is normal, do not start worrying even if he is little below average in weight.

Length/height

On an average, the ideal length of a full-term healthy infant at birth is 50 cms. It steps up to 60 cms at 3 months, 70 cms at 9 months, 75 cms at 1 year, 85 cms. at 4 years. Thereafter, the child gains a little over 5 cms every year until the onset of puberty.

As I remarked while talking about the weight, do not fuss if your child is a little shorter than the average figures, provided he is active, well and running about and provided that the doctor, after checking him up, says there is nothing wrong with him. Your child may be below average in weight and height but he can jolly well be a normal child.

Head size

Head circumference which reflects growth of the brain shows the following pattern of increase:

Birth—13 to 14 inches
6 months—16 inches
12 months—18 inches
3 years—19 inches
6 to 8 years—20 inches
10 to 12 years—21 inches (nearly adult size).

For your incidental interests, if the brain does not develop normally-as is the case in one type of mental retardation, the head size is likely to be small, the so-called *microcephaly*. Occasionally, the small size of the head may be due to premature union of the skull sutures. A large head may be the result of hydrocephalus or rickets.

Remember, a marginally large head (*macrocephaly*) may well be a family trait. It is just normal.

Teething (dentition)

The average age at which the first tooth appears is 6 to 7 months. The rest of the *milk teeth* appear at the rate of one tooth every month.

Thus, the number of teeth in an infant-age in months minus 6. By $2^1/_2$ to 3 years, the child has a full set of milk teeth numbering 20.

Generally, the lower central and the lateral incisors appear earlier followed by first molars, cuspids and second molars in succession.

The first permanent teeth—the so-called 6-year-molars—are sometimes confused with the temporary teeth. The pattern of eruption of temporary and permanent teeth is shown in the following tables.

Temporary Teething

Age	Eruption
Birth	None
6 to 7 months	First
By 10 months	Centrals and laterals
1 to $1\frac{1}{4}$ years	First molars
$1\frac{1}{4}$ to $1\frac{3}{4}$ years	Cuspids
2 to 3 years	Second molars

Permament Teething

Age	Eruption
6 years	First molars
8 years	Central and lateral incisors
9 years	Bicuspid (front)
10 years	Bicuspid (back)
11 to 12 years	Canines
12 to 13 years	Second molars
17 to 25 years	Third molars (wisdom teeth)

The number of temporary and permanent teeth is shown in the following table:

Number of Teeth

Temporary	$\dfrac{e\,d\,c\,b\,a \quad a\,b\,c\,d\,e}{e\,d\,c\,b\,a \quad a\,b\,c\,d\,e}$	20
Permanent	$\dfrac{8\,7\,6\,5\,4\,3\,2\,1 \quad 1\,2\,3\,4\,5\,6\,7\,8}{8\,7\,6\,5\,4\,3\,2\,1 \quad 1\,2\,3\,4\,5\,6\,7\,8}$	32

Important milestones at a glance

Social smile	6 weeks
Head holding	3 months
Sits with support	6 months
Sits without support	7 months
Reaches out for a bright object and gets it	5 to 6 months
Transfers object from one hand to the other	6 to 7 months
Starts imitating a cough	6 to 7 months
Crawls	8 to 10 months
Creeps	10 to 11 months
Stands holding furniture	9 months
Stands without support	10 to 11 months

Walks holding furniture	12 months
Walks without much of a support	13 months
Says one word with meaning	12 months
Says 3 words with meaning	12 months
Joins 2 or 3 words into a sentence	15 to 18 months
Feeds self with a spoon	13 months
Climbs stairs	15 to 18 months
Takes shoes and socks off	15 to 18 months
Puts shoes and socks on	2 years
Takes some clothes off	2 years
Dry by day	3 to 4 years
Dresses self fully	2 years
Dry by night	3 years
Knows full name and sex	3 years
Rides tricyle	3 years

16

VACCINATION (IMMUNISATION)

You may have heard about vaccination, immunisation or inoculation. What is it after all? Let us see.

The defence mechanism of the body is called *immunity*. It is of two types: natural and artifical. *Natural immunity* is purely a "gift from God", as Bertrand Russell once wrote. It may be limited to a particular species. Tetanus, a deadly disease characterised by lockjaw and rigidity of the body muscles, does not occur among the cattle though it is an important killer in humans.

When body defence or resistance to an infection is produced by introducing a protection from outside, it is called *artificial immunity*. When the protection is purely outside and short-lived—without participation of body's inside defence, the so-called *antibodies*—it is termed *passive immunity*. If, on the other hand, the outside protection creates in the body a storehouse of antibodies against a particular disease so that the body actively participates in resisting the infection, it is called *active immunity*. Unlike passive immunity, it lasts relatively longer.

So, production of artificial active immunity to safeguard against a particular disease by introducing an agent into the body through injections or orally is what is called *immunisation*. It is also termed *vaccination* or *inoculation*. The agent that is used to produce immunity is called vaccine.

Many mothers are concerned if vaccination really protects the child. Well, it does. In fact, it is the most practical and effective tool available with the doctors to protect against several communicable diseases. Once in a while, despite proper vaccination, the child may suffer from a particular infection. The disease in the child in such a situation is likely to be slight—at least much milder than what it would have been if the

vaccination had not been given at all. Obviously, even if the worst comes
to the worse, vaccination pays.

You must cooperate with your doctor in getting your child vaccinated
properly and in time. Just because it would take some of your time or cause
the child little pain or fever is no justification for neglecting this essential
component of child rearing. You should also educate other mothers in
your circle, as also in your neighbourhood about the preventive value of
vaccination in a simple but effective way.

I have frequently been bombarded by inquisitive women with a
question: "What are these booster doses? And Why?" Well, listen.

As I mentioned earlier in this very section, artificial active immunity
lasts relatively longer. To produce it, we give one or two (at times even
more) doses of a vaccine at definite intervals. This is called *primary
vaccination*. With the passage of time, the immunity so produced starts
decreasing. If, after a particular time lapse, another dose of the vaccine
is administered, it will go a long way to boost the effect of the initial
vaccination. This is the so-called *secondary vaccination* or *booster(s)*.
Remember not to forget it. It is not just the additional protection; it is an
essential part of immunisation.

Before I embark on the practical details about the individual
vaccinations, let me make it clear that what follows are the guidelines.
These are not a real substitute for the judgement and wisdom of your
doctor who knows your child and your circumstances the best. Also, do
not get puzzled if you find little variation in the recommendations from
centre to centre.

War on contagious diseases

Each year more than 80 million children are born in the developing world.
Each year about 5 million die from the contagious diseases. Reason? Just
less than 10 per cent are protected through vaccination. This does not
occur in the developed countries where protection is provided before the
first birthday.

In addition to those who die, many are disabled through brain
damage, paralysis, stunted growth, chronic lung disease, deafness or
blindness. Measles and whooping cough can also prevent a child from
eating and thus lead to malnutrition.

Think it over....None of this needs to happen.

Not just get your children protected against diphtheria, whooping cough, tetanus, poliomyelitis, measles and tuberculosis, spread the message to your friends and neighbours—in fact, to everyone you can contact.

National Immunisation Schedule

Beneficiaries	Age	Vaccine	No. of doses	Route of administration
Infants	6 weeks to 9 months	DPT	3	Intramuscular
	6 weeks to 9 months	Polio	3	Oral
	Birth to 3 months	BCG	1	Intradermal
	9 to 12 months	Measles	1	Subcutaneous
Children	18 to 24 months	DPT	1*	Intramuscular
	18 to 24 months	Polio	1*	Oral
	5 to 6 years	DT	1*	Intramuscular
	5 to 6 years	Typhoid	2	Subcutaneous
	10 years	TT	1**	Intramuscular
	10 years	Typhoid	1**	Subcutaneous
	16 years	TT	1**	Intramuscular
	16 years	Typhoid	1**	Subcutaneous
Pregnant Women	16 to 36 weeks	TT	1**	Intramuscular

* Booster doses
** 2 doses, if not vaccinated previously

Note: Interval between two doses should not be less than one month.
Minor coughs, colds and mild fever are not a contra-indication to vaccination.

BCG vaccination

B stands for Bacillus (a bacteria), C for Calmette and G for Guerin. Calmette and Guerin are the names of the two French scientists who developed this vaccine against tuberculosis in the early part of this century.

Whether this vaccine really protects has been a matter of hot controversy in recent years. You have perhaps read about it in the newspapers and magazines. To have a fresh look at the issue, the *Indian Academy of Pediatrics* held a National Workshop in New Delhi. The workshop was of the opinion that whereas there was a great deal of evidence that BCG offered definite protection against childhood tuberculosis, only very meagre evidence existed against this time-honoured concept. The experts strongly recommended that the present policy of giving BCG to every child be continued.

So, as your doctor would tell you, your child must get BCG as soon as possible after birth, preferably before he is 3 month old. Many centres do not in fact discharge the mother and the newborn unless the latter has received BCG

The standard site for giving BCG is the left shoulder. A very small needle and special tuberculin syringe are used to inject the vaccine into the skin. For mass vaccination the *jet injector* is of distinct value.

The vaccination is fairly safe. No fever is encountered. Leave the vaccination site as such. Do not apply dressing or antiseptic powder over it. In 2 to 3 weeks, a small elevation of the skin appears at the injection site. By about the fourth week, it grows in size. Then it either sheds into a shallow ulcer or disappears. The ulcer heals in about 8 weeks time, leaving a small scar.

Sometimes there may be noteworthy exceptions to the just described course of BCG vaccination. An accelerated response with a nodule or red-angry ulcer at the injection site after only 2 to 3 days and lasting about 3 weeks is noticed. Report it to the doctor. It is possible your child has already been having tuberculous infection.

Yet another category of infants develop a significant enlargement of glands in the armpit and/or neck. The swelling may progressively increase in size and start discharging pus. A medical consultation will be in order.

Lastly, there is some evidence that BCG also gives protection against leprosy (a progressive and contagious disease characterised by involvement of skin and nerves) and leukemia (a sort of blood cancer). Many child specialists are now making use of it in investigating suspected cases of tuberculosis.

Polio vaccination

Polio—poliomyelitis to be exact—is a leading cause of paralysis of the limbs and crippling in childhood.

Administration of oral polio vaccine in the form of a sweet tablet or drops, beginning at the age of 6 weeks, is a recognised means to protect against the disease. The vaccine is safe.

Most centres give three doses at 4 to 6 weeks' intervals. I may mention here that if your doctor wants to give 5 doses and your circumstances permit, follow his advice. He is doing so to have higher protection.

About the booster dose—well, it should be given 12 to 18 months after the last dose of the primary vaccine. It is of advantage to have another booster dose at the age of 5 years. Some doctors may like to give a booster dose every year until the age of 5 years and then every other year in subsequent childhood. Again, the aim is to accomplish the highest possible protection.

Vaccine should not be given as and when the baby is suffering from severe acute diarrhoea or a significant acute illness.

Another important point: a child who has earlier suffered from poliomyelitis is also a candidate for receiving full immunisation with the vaccine.

Triple (DPT) vaccination

This is a combined vaccine against diptheria, pertussis (whooping cough) and tetanus—the three diseases that are responsible for considerable ill-health and deaths in the child population of developing countries.

DPT vaccination is done at the same sittings as for polio vaccination. Beyond the age of 5 years, pertussis component in the vaccine is omitted. What is given is DT. This is because, before this age, complications of the pertussis component are far worse than the disease *per se*.

Triple vaccine is given as deep intramuscular injection over the external part of the thigh or the muscle mass of the upper arm. Within a few hours of the injection, fever develops in most babies and the baby may feel tenderness over the injection site. You may give him paracetamol and apply hot fomentation locally. If an injection abscess is formed, you must seek medical advice. Do not worry about the small lump that you may be able to feel at the injection site. It will disappear in 2 to 3 months.

Do not give the baby DPT vaccine if he is suffering from epilepsy and during a febrile illness. Mild diarrhoea or running nose are not contra-indications to its administration.

Measles vaccination

This vaccine is not yet freely available in developing regions and is expensive. Your doctor will like to give it to the baby by injection beween

9 and 12 months of age, or perhaps after that. A single injection produces immunity against measles for a prolonged period. Boosters are not required.

Among the various conditions in which the doctor may not like to give this vaccine rank any acute and fulminant illness, allergy, eczema, and convulsions.

The vaccine is quite safe provided due precautions are taken. At times, the baby may develop high fever and perhaps fits. At the time of vaccination, the doctor will guide you as to what to do if such complications occur.

Mumps vaccination

This vaccine is very effective against mumps. Only one injection is sufficient. It is very safe also. Unfortunately it is available in big cities only and is expensive.

Rubella vaccination

A single injection of this vaccine gives excellent protection against rubella or German measles. It is safe but expensive and not yet freely available in India. If you can procure it, remember that it is required to be given to the girls only, between 1 year of age and puberty.

MMR vaccination

This is a combination of measles, mumps and rubella vaccines—all in one. It is not easily available but if you can manage it, you need not give the three vaccines separately at all.

Typhoid vaccination

Your doctor will give it when the child is about 5-6 years of age. It is administered in two injections at a few weeks' intervals followed by boosters at 10 and 16 years. The month of March is the best time to give it. This will protect the child against typhoid and paratyphoid fevers when their season, that is summer, comes.

Occasionally, the child may develop local pain and fever following this vaccination. You may give him paracetamol in consultation with the doctor.

Cholera vaccination

Except under special circumstances and travel to certain countries, cholera vaccination need not be given.

Children under five years require 2 doses. Just one dose suffices for older children. This gives protection for 3 to 6 months.

The vaccine may cause local pain and fever which respond favourably to paracetamol.

Influenza vaccination

Currently this vaccine has got to be imported. Given as a subcutaneous (under the skin) injection, it protects against influenza, the so-called *flu*.

17

TOILET TRAINING

Ninety per cent babies begin to develop voluntary (intentional) control over bladder and bowel between 1 year to $2^1/_2$ years. In a large proportion, it occurs between $1^1/_2$ years to 2 years. The baby usually gives a signal in the form of a gesture (say a grunt) or a family word such as *su-su* or *chi-chi*. The alert mother finds no difficulty in understanding that the child wants to pass motion or urine.

The whole thing does not happen just overnight. To begin with, he indicates to his mother that he has soiled his nappie. Later, he tells her in his own way as and when he is in the process of soiling it. Still later, he indicates to her that he is just about to wet it. Eventually, he manages to indicate to her that he wishes to do so and gives her time to sort things out. After this stage has arrived—which happens usually by 2 years of age— he can be relied upon to tell the mother "in time" about his approaching "movement". However, before fully depending upon his signal, she should continue reminding him if he wants to pass motion or urine from time to time over quite a few months. This way very many accidents can be avoided, especially on account of his forgetfulness while being very busy in play or some such thing.

By the age of $2^1/_2$ years, most babies will pull their pants down as soon as they find the urge to urinate or défaecate round the corner. They are more or less dry at night though accidental "wetting" may occur until the age of 5 years.

In general bladder control comes a few months later than bowel control. It is not so difficult for a child to control a movement as to control urine. Most 2-year-olds have complete control of movements; several children are still wetting during day or night at $2^1/_2$ years of age, however.

Then, I have time and again been asked, how come some babies have learnt to be clean when they are hardly a few months old. To understand this, imagine a baby being put on the outstretched legs of the mother or on the pottie regularly. He is likely to learn the habit to urinate or defaecate at the feel of the legs of the mother or the rim of the pottie or perhaps just the special gesture or sound the mother makes. This is not intentional or voluntary effort on the part of the child. It is just that he has been conditioned to it. He may do it when put in this position even during sound sleep. I have seen many sophisticated mothers successfully putting 3 or 4 month-old babies on pottie.

"When should I begin his pottie training?" is an oft-asked question by young mothers. Should it be when the baby is 2 to 3 months old? Will the age of around 9 months when the baby can sit properly and securely be all right? Or, should she wait until the baby starts communicating to her that he has an urge to pass stool or urine?

I am of the opinion that what indeed matters in toilet training is not the age at which you initiate it but how you accomplish it. Never force him to sit on the pottie. Else he will trouble you with behaviour problems later. Also, do not press him to sit on it for too long. On an average a sitting of a few minutes is enough. Whether or not he has passed anything, let him get off if he wishes to. If the child indeed resists sitting on the pottie, forget it for the time being. Perhaps you can try again after a gap of a week or so. It is one front on which your fussiness and persistence will only backfire. Take it easy. That is what will eventually pay.

Another important point: do not feel discouraged because your child has taken longer time to be adequately trained than your neighbour's child. Do not forget no two children are the same. What works fine for one may not be all right for another. So, have patience. Make enough use of encouragement rather than force and disapproval in training your child.

If you are a believer in early training, I would suggest that you start putting the baby on pottie any time between 7 and 12 months provided that the baby has movements at the same time of the day. At this age he has developed little voluntary control and can sit comfortably and securely. It will be a good preparation for training if not the real training. But, mind you, it is unwise to try this schedule if the baby's movement is irregular. You will not know when he is to pass motion. To make him sit on the pottie so frequently will mean testing his patience which is most undesirable. You will only be nurturing a rebellion in the mind of the little man.

The most natural age to put the child on the pottie seems to be the second half of the second year. This is the age at which he may show more interest in the pottie and may, in fact, give a signal of the approaching movement or urination. You must encourage him to give you a signal. Praise him for signalling today. Encourage him to tell you again tomorrow, the day-after-tomorrow and everyday. Do not scold him for an accidental soiling of clothes.

Buy an attractive plastic pottie for your baby. Let him play with it, get friendly with it and sit on it. You may suggest that it is meant to have a movement but do not try to force him to use it for this purpose. More often that not, the baby will grow fond of it. This will become his proud possession. Someday he may well begin to pass motion in it.

Difficulties in bowel control

During the bowel training period, see that the child does not get constipated. Unusually hard stools—especially one large piece with a big diameter—may cause pain. At times, such a movement can result in a tear of the anus, the so-called *anal fissure* which is quite painful and takes a long time to heal. Such a child may attempt to hold back his movement lest it causes further pain. What results is still harder stool. A vicious cycle is set up. Look up the doctor for advice. On your part, see that the child receives enough of fluids and juice in his daily diet to safeguard against hard stools. Avoid the use of laxatives or purgatives.

If a trained child becomes irregular, consult the doctor. It is possible he has developed an infection—say diarrhoea. Teething, emotional upset, change of surroundings, and jealousy are some other factors that may cause relapse in a child who has once learnt control. Do not scold or rebuke him. Instead, encourage him in a friendly manner to tide over the "gulf" and return to normalcy again in due course.

Do not lose your temper if your small baby fiddles with his stools and perhaps puts a bit of these into his mouth. Remember, he does not know that these are, as you would like to put it, "nothing but filth". All that he knows is that these are his very own. He would certainly be interested in exploring these like he explores everything. Soon he will grow out of it.

Then, there are babies who suddenly change their pattern after having used the pottie over several months. Such a child starts holding the movement as long as he sits on the pottie. No sooner does he get away from the seat, than he moves his bowel in a corner of the room or perhaps in his panties. Do not try to be cross and bossy; that will only aggravate the situation. Psychologists believe that this phenomenon results from the fact that the child has begun to think his stools are a part of his body and he wishes to hold on to his possession more obstinately. Moreover, he wishes to do everything in his own way in the second year of life. Assertive types of boys show it most frequently. They love fuss and the entire family revolving round their movements. This is one way they try to demonstrate their importance. You should not evince much interest in his refusal to sit on the pottie and should not scold or punish him. A wise change in management, needing a shift in tactics and lots of patience over weeks and at times months, will most likely bring about a *positive* response.

Soiling

You should remember that your overenthusiastic attitude towards potting may lead to soiling in infancy. Another cause of soiling, especially if it develops after a period of bowel control, is emotional instability and insecurity. But, experience has shown that if soiling occurs after the age of 3 or 4 years, chances are that the child is constipated. The child passes liquid material (around solid faecal lumps, the so-called *faecolith*) intermittently through the anus, thereby wetting his panties and the like. What I would like to stress again is that you should not let the child's constipation go on and on. Prevent it but if it occurs willy-nilly, consult your doctor. Maybe he prescribes half a teaspoonful of Milk of Magnesia or liquid paraffin. Suppositories, purgatives and enemas are rarely, if ever, needed.

Difficulties in bladder control

Most children learn to be dry during the day at the age of 2 years; by 3 years, they are dry by night too.

Some children deliberately ask for the pottie every few minutes; others urinate after getting off the pottie. Yet another group of children deliberately hold back urine for a considerable time. All these may well be attention-seeking behaviour problems.

I do not think it is necessary for parents to do anything special to correct these. You will be treating these best by just "ignoring". But do not forget to seek medical advice if there is a suspicion of a disease. If the child, for instance, starts passing urine excessively, make sure he does not have urinary tract infection. Your doctor will need a urine sample to examine and to tell you if it is an infection or not.

Occasionally, your child may have constant dribbling of urine every minute. Your doctor will certainly like to investigate the child for a malformation which is generally correctable by surgery.

Excessive frequency of urine in association with excessive thirst and voracious appetite could well be a manifestation of diabetes mellitus. There is wisdom in bringing it to the notice of the doctor.

Enuresis (Bed-wetting)

In my experience about 25 per cent children fail to acquire bladder control after the age of 3 years. Such a child does not just wet his bed at night; he fails to wait when he gets an urge to pass urine even during daytime. Boys suffer more often than girls. In a considerable proportion of cases, there is family history of such a problem—in father, in mother or in the siblings. We doctors call the condition *enuresis*. Since the bed-wetting usually occurs during night, it is also known as *nocturnal enuresis*.

The cause of enuresis is not always clear—in fact, it is only infrequently precisely defined. Physical factors like threadworm infestation, infection of external genitals or urinary tract and anatomical defects in urinary tract are responsible in some of the cases.

Too late or improper bladder training by the parents is also an important contributing factor.

A general consensus is that enuresis may be a manifestation of family conflict and maladjustment—that is, too strict parents, rejection, jealousy or rivalry among children. An erratic handling of the problem by the parents causes further anxiety to the child. His condition, therefore, gets more aggravated.

Your doctor, when contacted, will interview you as also the child to find the causative—at least accompanying emotional—factors. A complete physical check-up as also urine and stool examination, X-ray of lower spine to rule out urinary tract infection, threadworm infestation or anatomical defects may be ordered by him. Treatment of the underlying disease will cure enuresis.

But, as I said earlier, in a large majority of cases no definite cause is forthcoming. Encouragement and not scolding is the most important measure that is going to be of value. You should boost him to have dry nights. In fact he should be offered a special pat and even reward on such occasions when he does not wet the bed. Also, protect the mattress by waterproof sheeting.

Restrict too much of fluids, including tea and coffee, in the evening, especially towards bedtime. Insist on his voiding before retiring to bed.

You should make it a point to wake him up once or twice during the night and make sure that he voids.

If the child is a 5-year-old or above, you may make use of a device, an *electric buzzer*, which is designed in such a way that the child wakes up from noise as soon as the special pad on which he sleeps is wet by a few drops of urine. The device is based on condition reflex response and is marketed. This technique requires a trial for 3 months or longer.

Most doctors will prescribe a tablet of imipramine *(Depsonil)* or amitryptyline *(Tryptanol)* at bedtime for about 6 to 8 weeks. Some will supplement it with a small dose of diazepam *(Calmpose* or *Valium)*.

Whatever line of management your doctor suggests for the child, remember that you should never let the child feel guilty. Never put him to shame by scolding him, especially in the presence of guests. A certain mother got into the habit of firing her 5-year-old in these words: "You creep, you have been getting on my nerves. You'll never stop that, I suppose." Little wonder, the child was too glad to oblige her; his bed-wetting continued until he was 10.

For the child who wets during daytime too what is most important in management is the positive parental attitude. Train him to hold out as long as possible as and when he feels like urinating. This way he will be able to train his bladder to hold more before it empties.

Finally, even at the cost of repetition, I must say that impatience, insecurity, anxiety and too rigid parental attitudes are the solid bottlenecks in the successful management of enuresis. You should review the family situation as also do some heart-searching if your child has had such a problem.

18

CARE OF THE TEETH

While discussing growth and development in Chapter 15, I had talked about eruption of temporary (milk) and permanent teeth. Let us now see how you should take care of the child's dental health.

Brushing

Do not wait that the child would grow up and then start brushing his teeth. He will, of course, do that when he is a 2-year-old. But, before that, you should wipe his teeth with a lint and a soft brush. Yes, everyday.

As soon as he is 2 years of age, teach him to brush his teeth himself after eating and before retiring to bed. Impress upon him the significance of brushing. Tell him how it helps to maintain their cleanliness and improve their appearance.

It is important to teach him the correct way of brushing the teeth. Just a small quantity of toothpaste suffices. It is wrong to brush across the teeth. Brush, on the other hand, in the direction of their growth—up in the case of lower teeth and down in the case of upper teeth. Brush should be used in rotating movements. The back of the teeth as also the cutting edges should also be properly brushed.

Many mothers wonder if the child would take to brushing the teeth easily. He will. Two years is an age at which he is inclined to imitate all that the elders do around him. Watching his parents brushing their teeth, he one day catches hold of a brush, fiddles with it and then tries it on his own teeth. Buy him a soft brush. Encourage him to master the technique of brushing which would, of course, take time.

Remember not to let the child use a wornout toothbrush. A bad brush does no good. Instead, it may damage his delicate gums. There is some sense in hanging toothbrushes in the bathroom as well as in the dining room, close to the washbasin.

Do not neglect nutrition

The part of the teeth that strikes the eye is what is called a *crown*. The mother's diet during pregnancy has a great bearing on the formation of the crown of the milk teeth. If you had had adequate calcium, phosphorous, fluoride, vitamin C and vitamin D, chances are that your baby's teeth will be strong. Remember, injudicious use of such drugs as tetracyclines during pregnancy can cause staining of the infant's teeth.

Not that the baby's own nutrition is not important. It is. Make sure that he gets enough of calcium and phosphorus (milk is a rich source of both) as also vitamins C and D during the years the child's teeth are being formed.

How to avoid dental decay

Dental decay or *caries* is by far the commonest disease of teeth. No one knows for sure as to what actually causes it. Experts believe that heredity plays some role. Nutritional inadequacy seemingly plays a part. What, I believe, matters most in its causation is the excessive use of sugar. Add to it the bad dental hygiene—that is the child's carelessness to brush the teeth regularly so that particles of food remain clung to the teeth or between them.

The food particles lead to caries by excessive production of lactic acid by the bacteria which feed on sugar and starch. This acid dissolves the outer covering of the teeth, producing small holes or cavities. The cavities allow further lodging of the food particles which will mean greater bacterial growth leading to further production of lactic acid and enlargement of cavities from further destruction of teeth. A vicious circle is set up.

The worst offender among various sugar foods are candies, chocolates, toffees, lollipops, cookies, crackers, dry fruits and the like—anything sugary that sticks to the teeth. A dummy containing a sweet stuff or dipped in it is also very damaging to the child's teeth.

So, remember not to encourage the child to go in for sweets day in and day out. The sugar provided by fruits such as apple is dilute and is washed away easily. It may, in fact, help to cleanse the teeth. In any case, make sure that debris does not remain clung to the teeth. It may not be possible to brush the teeth after every eating session, but it is certainly not difficult to rinse the mouth properly.

Do not delay to see the dentist if the child complains of a sensation of cold after taking a cold drink or ice cream, if he has toothache or if you detect a mark of decay in a tooth. It is of advantage to get filling done in a cavity irrespective of whether it is a temporary or permanent tooth. Do not ignore a bad temporary tooth. It may have to be removed if not cared for in time. That is likely to cause eruption of the permanent tooth in an undesirable position.

Dental overcrowding can be checked

Overcrowding of teeth looks dirty. It makes the teeth more vulnerable to collection of food particles and thus eventually to dental decay.

It is advisable to have a regular dental check-up of the child after the age of 3 years. A visit to the dentist every 6 months is quite in order. Not only will he find out and fill if any cavity is formed, he will also be able to check any malocclusion of teeth. Remember, today he can even correct malocculsion.

Tooth reimplantation

In case an injury dislodges the child's tooth, make sure to preserve the tooth in a wet cotton cloth and to look up a good dentist immediately, within an hour or two. It is quite possible he succeeds in replacing it back in its position.

19

THE BABY WHO CRIES AND CRIES

"Look at this little rascal. He has been crying and crying and would sure drive me mad," said a young sophisticated mother, drawing my attention to her 2-month-old infant, the other day.

Well, excessive crying is quite a common problem in small children. Though in majority of the cases its cause is minor (at times it may not be clear), the baby who cries a lot may leave the mother tense, exhausted and bored. One such mother told me in Simla a few years back: "At times she gets so much on my nerves that I really feel like throwing her out of the window." She added: "After a day's hard work, you do need sleep. Don't you? Imagine then our predicament when her continuous crying bores us to death."

Looking for the cause

Why do babies cry? Most mothers (in fact, both parents and even other family members) would like to know the reason(s) so that they can find the remedial measures.

Hunger cry: This is by far the most common cause of periodical crying. The younger the baby, the greater are the chances of his crying for the feed. One hungry baby may wait to make a fuss while another may immediately start screaming and crying, not stopping until he is fed.

Experience has demonstrated that if the mother is fairly sure that it is far too early to give him the feed (perhaps she gave a good one just an hour back), she is well advised to refrain from offering the breast or the bottle. All that may stop his crying is to be picked up and fondled.

Yet, very often some mothers—including the educated ones—wonder why the baby should cry for feed when they have been giving an adequate quantity of it. A good proportion of them have poor idea about a growing baby's requirements. Some just do not really know how to prepare the formula. One such mother, a lecturer in a college, was recently found adding 100 per cent water to her 3-month-old's feeds. What she was feeding to the infant was all right as far as the total quantity of the feed was concerned. However, it contained just half of the recommended quantity of milk. Good reason for his crying and crying and his growth failure!

You are well advised to avoid diluted cow's milk for the baby. Also, don't ever overdilute the baby milk powder. Prepare the formula as per instructions printed on the tin or in the leaflet that you may find inside it. If, however, your doctor has advised you otherwise, that makes an entirely different story. He knows your baby best. Better follow his instructions.

Thirst crying: Just as too diluted a feed causes hunger crying, a highly concentrated formula may cause excessive thirst crying, especially in early days.

Erratic feeding technique: Some mothers just do not know that feeding too is a technique. They feed the child in such a position that proximity of the breast almost blocks the baby's nose.

Yet another group of inexperienced mothers do not properly kick the wind out, the so-called *burping*, after feeding the baby. The wind in the stomach causes discomfort and crying. The cry of such a baby is in the form of high-pitched screams. Crying in this situation leads to inhalation of further wind. A vicious cycle of *wind-crying-wind-crying* is thereby set in.

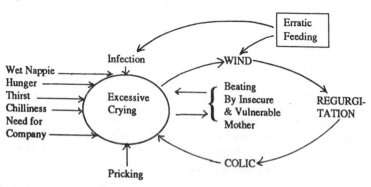

Vicious Cycle of Excessive Crying

Need for company: Little ones need love and company. Their resentment against "loneliness" is well-founded. All that such a baby can do to express his disgust is to cry. Crying will stop when he is picked up, more so by the mother who does nearly everything for him and to whom he is rightly attached.

I have frequently been asked if it is fair to pick up the baby when he cries and asks for it. I feel it is quite fair—in fact, eminently desirable.

Won't it turn him into a spoilt child? Won't it be a faulty upbringing? Most authorities hold that picking up and loving the baby in moderation will make him more secure and less demanding in later years. As Ronald Illingworth puts it, "mothers who are most careful to avoid spoiling are often the possessers of children who are horribly spoiled and insecure." Such children cling to their mother's legs far too long— "long after other children have learnt independence and more mature behaviour."

Discomfort: A wet or soiled nappie usually troubles an infant, causing crying. Let the mother make him clean and dry and change the nappie. All too soon, he becomes quiet.

Overclothing and underclothing also may cause the child to cry.

At times crying is secondary to something pricking the baby. In the winter of 1971, I was approached by a young lady whose 3-month-old son would scream restlessly every night. This had been going on and on for about a week or so. There was no obvious cause I could find. When I visited their house in a posh locality of Chandigarh, I was surprised to see how small negligences could lead to troubles. There were quite a few *all-pins* stuck into the little blanket that was being used for the baby at night. In the subsequent years I have found similar situations on more than twenty occasions.

Teething: Eruption of teeth is a painful process, making some babies exceedingly irritable. They may cry a lot. Eruption of the back teeth may be accompanied by earache. I have often come across mothers rushing to ENT specialists in such cases. No doubt, ears are found to be normal. Yet, it is a good policy to rule out ear problem before ascribing earache to teething.

Tiredness: Most babies sleep after getting exhausted. Some react differently. They, particularly the ones beyond three months of age, may cry and cry and refuse the feed. Such a baby needs gentle fondling and rocking before he agrees to fall asleep.

Boredom: At five months of age, the baby may not like to continue to lie flat. Propped up position, enabling him to see what is happening in the surroundings, usually helps to quieten him. Changing the position and making available something to see are, therefore, strongly recommended in growing infants.

Three months colic: Some babies during the first three months of life experience a sharp tummy pain towards the evening. The baby is usually healthy. No specific underlying cause has so far been found. It is possible that "wind in the stomach" or certain "foods" have some role to play in its causation. If your baby has a problem, you may note if any food aggravates or causes it and accordingly avoid it.

The important thing for the family and the mother to bear in mind is that undue anxiety would only lead to further panic.

Still, if you feel the child is very much in distress, approaching the doctor will be quite in order. Maybe the baby needs a tranquilliser or a little sedation.

Habit crying: Some babies take mothers for a ride and develop the habit of crying in the hope that they would be picked up at the slightest pretext. Once you are convinced of the habit of crying, you must put your foot down. It is difficult to break it but, with firmness and determination, you are bound to be a success. Do not get disheartened.

Personality trait: A certain proportion of crying in children is perhaps related to "personality". The child has no idea of what he wants. He does not know what is wrong. All that he knows is that life is tough going. And, so he cries.

How far mother's own anxiety, tension and nervousness contribute to such crying is not clear. Nor is the role of naughtiness, spoiling, temper or habit formation as yet understood in its causation.

Battering: As a mother you may not like it but the fact is that some cruel parents treat an unwanted child badly. There are cases of little daughters having been beaten and starved. I know of a 9-month-old who was brought to the hospital for excessive crying and with a black-eye which was ascribed by the father to a fall. On examination, I found several old injuries including those of the bones. X-rays confirmed the presence of healing fractures. The father later admitted having mercilessly beaten the child on several occasions in the recent past. The parents had eight issues in total. All were daughters. They were particularly upset that the child under reference also turned out to be a girl.

Sickness: A common cause of abdominal pain and crying in the second half of the first year is the presence of worms in the intestines. In most parts of our country, roundworm, threadworm, giardia, hookworm, amoeba and dwarf tapeworm are very common in children. Your doctor would like to have one or more stool examination of the child to confirm or rule out this possibility. Treatment is quite simple but you should leave it to the doctor's advice. Self-medication can be dangerous.

Also, look for painful sores, boils or rashes which may be responsible for crying.

Acute infections such as upper respiratory infection, rhinitis (nose inflammation) or otitis (ear infection) or stomach upset need consultation from the doctor.

Avoid dummies and pacifiers

If you have been asked by a friend or the grandmother of the baby to resort to the use of pacifiers and dummies to calm down the crying child, just wait. You are being led up the garden path. These articles are no substitute for your love and fondling. In addition, there is risk of their introducing infection into the baby's mouth. Also, malocclusion and/or caries in front teeth may result.

If you are an honest and loving mother, do not expose your baby to all these risks just because you want to relax. He needs you, not the dummy.

20

THE WORKING MOTHER AND HER PROBLEMS

A doctor friend tells me that she is determined not to go in for a job until her 5 months old baby crosses his third birthday.

My hat's off to her! For, what she has planned is simply ideal for the child. It is during the first three years of life that the child needs the mother most to satisfy his physical and emtional needs. If she holds a full-time job, it is but natural that she would be disappearing from the house for the whole day at least during the weekdays. This may seriously disturb the child, causing what we doctors call *separation anxiety*. To say that a substitute may take the place of the real mother at this stage is simply imagining too much.

But what seems ideal may well be just not workable in the case of lots of women who have got to work and earn out of necessity. The number of such working women is steadily increasing. For, if the husband's income is not supplemented in these days of price hike and cut-throat competition, proper housing, clothing, food and other amenities for the family will not be forthcoming.

If you are a working woman but have an understanding mother-in-law or some other woman in the family, she can prove a boon to the baby while you are away at the office etc. Else, you will need a maidservant to look after the baby. Before taking such a baby-sitter in your employment make sure that she is good-natured, affectionate to the baby and well-versed in baby care. Her habits should be clean and hygienic. She should not be suffering from any such disease as skin problem, intestinal worm infestation or tuberculosis. Mind you, a bad ayah may prove a nuisance rather than useful to the baby and the family.

If you have a creche in your neighbourhood, you may leave the baby there while you are away. Ensure that the creche is really dependable, otherwise your baby may suffer.

I keep hearing many young women grumbling that as full-time workers they are dog-tired by the time they return home. Then, there is too much of work back home. To cap that all, they are supposed to look after the baby as well. The result: it is the baby who suffers most. All I can say is that when it is work that is interfering with the care of the child, you must discuss things with the husband and other elders in the family. Chances are that a via media will be found so that you can take time off to look after the "little one". Remember that there is no alternative to your spending time with the baby. Avoid reading thrillers and excessive socialising when the child is young.

The question of breast-feeding

Just because you are working is a bad reason for stopping the healthy practice of breast-feeding your baby. Most organisations provide maternity leave, 6 weeks each before and after the delivery. Just a few days before resuming your work, you may gradually replace the day's feeds with the bottle. This would mean giving the child just two bottle feeds. In the morning and after returning from work, you should continue giving your own feeds.

21

THE GROWING CHILD AND "FATHERING"

The readers would recall that in Chapter 3, I had stressed the strong need for the active support of the father-to-be to the mother-to-be while she was busy dreaming beautiful dreams etc., while carrying the baby in her tummy.

My wife, who was kind enough to go through the manuscript at the prepublication stage and offer suggestions, shot back: "But how about the husband's continued support to the spouse in the later years—I mean after the arrival of the child and in the course of his subsequent growing-up and the like? You surely do not mean raising the child is entirely the mother's job now that we are endeavouring into the twentieth century?"

Needless to say, the point was very well taken. So, here I take off...

Let me start by putting it across to you that the father's role by no means ends with the delivery. On the contrary, it finds further extension in a "big way" as the baby arrives and grows from one phase to another. You may call it "fathering", or as the noted pediatric teacher, the late Professor S.S. Manchanda, liked to designate it "modified mothering". To be frank, it is extremely difficult to draw a cut-off line between the role of the mother and that of the father in the care of the child. A lot of overlap is inevitable, depending on such factor(s) as whether both parents are working.

The father, as the noted World Health Organization expert, Professor Michael Gray, puts it in a recent issue of the *World Health*, must consider care of the child as vital as his job or career. I am in total agreement with this point of view.

I strongly feel that the father must actively—and, of course, equally—contribute to all aspects of home and childcare, especially if the lady is holding an outside job. He is not supposed to do so on compassionate grounds, out of generosity or as a favour to the better-half, but in the true spirit of equal partnership which is the backbone of a successful family life. A particular gentleman would return home and speak to his wife in terms such as this: "Our new friend must have exhausted you to the bone. So, let me assist you here.... And, don't forget to feel grateful for this out-of-the-way help. Understand?" Such an attitude of the hubby, undoubtedly, defeats the very purpose of the assistance rendered. Worse, it may well backfire, causing additional problems.

More often than not, the father postpones taking share of the child's care till the little one grows a little. This way valuable time is lost and before long the mother becomes an expert in taking care of the child whereas the father is still planning and postponing "fathering".

You may well question: how does the father's sharing care of the child and home help? First, as you can appreciate, it decidedly lightens the wife's load. Secondly, it gives her a badly-needed companionship, more so in situations concerning nuclear families. Thirdly, it provides the child with a variety of styles of leadership and control. Consequent upon that, he grows up without any kind of sexist attitudes. Fourthly, it gives the mother mental contentment. The observation that her hubby believes that raising the child is a responsibility of both the partners and that sharing is crucial for the welfare of the child means a great lot to her.

What kinds of work can the father do? On the home front, he can help his spouse in shopping, bedmaking, laying the table and perhaps in cooking. As far as the child is concerned, the father can contribute to his care in feeding, changing nappies/dress, bathing, washing the pottie, putting to bed and playing etc. For a somewhat older child, he can read stories, teach discipline, break up quarrels and help in doing homework etc.

While re-emphasizing that father's positive help in bringing up the child adds to the latter's security and development, let me tell you that the father's role after the child has attained the age of two years becomes more important. The child is eager to imitate the father. This tendency for "identification" must be encouraged. To ensure that this tendency proves gratifying, the father must be in command, a sort of balanced authority whom, as far as possible, everybody obeys. In no case should the father try to be authoritarian, asserting himself roughly over the child and the wife. Such authoritarianism, in fact, invites troubles inasmuch as that the child either becomes "inhibited" or "rebellious". There is a good deal of evidence that an authoritarian father quite often had emotional difficulties in his early childhood. This is an excellent example of "fizzled out" or "negative" fathering. The sooner it is stopped, the better.

A word about the "weak" father. Such a father is far too submissive to be a model with whom the child can identify. It is just the opposite of what we just finished talking about, i.e. authoritarian father. This situation too leads to many adjustment problems, anxiety and insecurity in the child, more so in the teenager.

In case of divorce or death, the father may have to single-handedly take care of the child. This kind of "single parenting" can cause problems. For instance, the daughter, because of non-availability of the mother, may get too intimate with the father. This may result in difficulties when she reaches puberty. Secondly, since the father gets obsessed with the child's upbringing, there may result a lack of security of his authority.

Then, there is the father with a wife who is far-too possessive or authoritarian (a sort of mirror image of his mother). Such a father fails to provide the child tranquillity, security and stability that the child needs so badly.

Finally, let me wind up with the remarks (yes, even at the risk of repetition) that a happy relationship, partnership and harmony between the parents are the vital and precious stabilising influences for the healthier upbringing of the child. The father's share need not, in any significant way, be less in this important field.

22

ACCIDENTS AND THEIR PREVENTION

Accidents, within the home premises or in the street, are a common cause of disability and death in our young children.

Remember, accidents in children occur

a. Mostly at home;
b. More often when mothering is being done by someone else;
c. Mostly in early childhood, especially after the first birthday;
d. More frequently at the time of the mother's periods;
e. More frequently in overprotected and least-exposed children;
f. More frequently in children who lack discipline.

Accident prevention requires three things. First is the *forethought* which means to think of and become sensitive to this possible risk to the child. Secondly, *time* in order to watch the child and his activities. Thirdly, *discipline* which should be well-balanced.

You must remember that as long as the child has not crossed his first birthday, providing him total protection is your responsibility and duty. Do maintain relatively less protection against accidents in later years but also expose him to have the feel of minor troubles, such as a little fall from a chair, heat of a teapot or a pin-prick. How else will the child learn valuable lessons? The best protection against drowning is to teach him swimming and water safety rather than keep him away from water.

Calendar of Accident Proneness

Birth to 6 months

Needs full time protection; towards the fag-end of this age range, baby grasps and moves, making accidents more prone.

6 to 12 months

Sits, crawls, stands and may begin walking; takes everything to mouth; pulls himself up and all else down.

1 to 2 years

Occupied in exploration; climbs, opens drawers and doors; likes to play in water.

2 to 3 years

Imitates; likes to do everything all alone; impatient with restraint.

3 to 6 years

Explores the neighbourhood; climbs, rides tricycle and bicycle; plays rough games; often moves out of sight; responds to consistent advice about what can be dangerous for him.

Cuts, locations and trapping of fingers

Sharp objects such as blades, scissors, opened tins, knives, forks, nails and certain poor-quality playthings must neither be left about nor children permitted to run about with them.

Likewise discourage children from playing door-banging games, from closing doors with lots of force. You too should set an example by opening and closing doors gently. Always watch that the child's fingers do not get trapped while you close the door.

If an injury, however, results, you should clean the wound with soap and water or, if available, with an antiseptic solution. It will be advisable to see the doctor also as soon as possible, especially if the wound is large. It is possible the cut needs stitches. Your doctor may like to give the child tetanus toxoid, some tablets to kill the pain and an antibiotic cover to prevent the occurrence of infection.

Falls

In a small infant's case, keep the railing of the cot up. As soon as he is old enough to climb out of the cot, put him to bed.

Never allow the child to play on the stairs, more so on its railing.

Do not let any greasy stuff stay on the floor long enough to make it slippery.

Place furniture in such a manner that children do not climb over it to look out of the window and then have nasty falls. It is good to have a safe high chair.

Discourage children from kite-flying from the housetops. In north India, many fatal falls occur this way.

Always report to the nearest hospital's casualty department if the child gets a fracture, a large wound or becomes unconscious following a fall.

Burns

The child may get burns from spilling of hot soup, water, tea, coffee or milk. He may start playing with a low-level stove in the kitchen and burn himself. Never allow the child to play with matchsticks or fireworks. Never let him get into the practice of climbing into the fireplace to recover a plaything. It is dangerous to have a mirror above the fireplace. He may like to look at himself and allow his clothes to catch fire.

Make sure that your child doesn't turn on the hot tap.

Make sure that your child does not wear garments of such inflammable synthetic material as will easily catch fire.

Remember it is risky to hold the baby in your lap and then sip hot tea or coffee.

Never leave a hot-water bottle in your child's bed.

Never place hot tea or coffee-pot close to the edge of the table. Also ensure that the tablecloth does not hang over the edge of the table. The child may pull the cloth, bringing the hot stuff over him.

If the burn is minor, you may look up the doctor at his convenience but if it is extensive you must rush the child to the hospital immediately.

Drowning

Never leave the baby alone in the bath; the child may slip in the tub and get drowned.

Teach the child swimming as soon as he is old enough. Also, never forget to accompany small children while swimming.

It is dangerous to allow small children in a boat without a life-jacket.

Electrocution

To ensure against electric shock, see that the electric points in the walls are high enough to prevent children putting their fingers into them.

Also, remember to unplug an electric equipment when it is no longer in use.

Always avoid having an electric fire in the bathroom.

Keep the child out of the way when using electric wringers, mixers or sewing machines.

Suffocation

Never play with the child who has food in his mouth.

Never allow the child to play with a cord round the neck or plastic or other bags put over the head.

Always discourage the child from playing in a cupboard or refrigerator.

Wait, Pacifiers can be Dangerous

According to a study conducted by the *Child Health Study Group*, 80 million pacifiers are sold annually in India.

There have been several instances of choking and death involving pacifiers, in India and abroad. New regulations in the USA stipulate that guard or shield be part of the pacifier, of sufficient size so that the entire pacifier cannot be drawn into the child's mouth. The shield must also have at least two ventilation holes to facilitate breathing if the pacifier gets swallowed.

No pacifier in the States can be sold with a ribbon string, cord or similar item attached to it. All pacifiers must be labelled:

Warning:Do not put the pacifier around the child's neck as it presents a strangulation danger.

Should you see a pacifier (better avoid it), bear the hazard in mind. Take adequate precautions. If the warning is addressed to American mothers, it indeed holds good in your case as well.

Poisons

Keep all medicines, pesticides, disinfectants, cleansing agents—in fact, all poisons—out of the child's reach, under lock and key.

It is advisable to label all bottles, like "kerosene oil" or "turpentine oil."

All discarded medicines need destruction rather than a lazy waiting for the occasion to come when these may be reused.

Never tell the child that the pill is a sweet. Refer to the medicine as medicine.

Never give wax crayons to a small child. These are likely to be chewed by him, causing poisoning.

Avoid painting of your walls with lead paint. Many children are fond of eating the paint flakes.

Also, do not leave the batteries of a torch light outside. Your child may get lead poisoning.

Foreign bodies

It is natural for a curious child to pick up coins, marbles, buttons, nuts, beads, pins—in fact, anything that comes his way—into his mouth, nose or ears.

Fortunately, most of the time, as we have seen, the foreign body goes into the digestive tract and is passed out in the stool without causing any damage.

That doesn't, however, always happen. If it gets into the air passage, it may choke the child to death.

A foreign body in the nose or ear may cause problems later on. These include bleeding and local sepsis.

The best course is not to let such objects be within a child's reach. Also teach him not to put them into the mouth, ear or nose. Don't allow him to run and eat at the same time. Hard foods can easily be caught in the throat. If you suspect the child has taken a foreign body in, always consult an Ear, Nose, Throat Specialist. Do not try to heroically remove it yourself; you may only aggravate things.

Traffic accidents

Never allow the child to play in streets.

He should be taught how to safely cross the road as soon as he is old enough.

He should be careful not to be run over by a reversing car.

Never allow the child to stand in a car when in motion and never leave the child alone in the car unless you have made sure that the keys are with you.

Caution the child against ditches and manholes in the drive which may cause accidents if the child is on a bicyle or tricycle.

Why not update your safety plan?

All said and done, remember that children do keep having accidents. Yet, most come out without any significant problems. So, all that we talked about accidents need not frighten you. On the contrary, it should inspire you to update your safety plan.

Let us see how you answer these queries:

1. Do you have first aid kit for burns, cuts and falls, poisons etc?
2. Is your house properly fenced from the street and do the risky sides having adequate grill etc?
3. Are you satisfied that your medicines and dangerous household cleaners are properly stored?
4. Are you satisfied that your garden tools are properly stored?
5. Are you satisfied with your electric wiring, connections and points?
6. Are you satisfied with the safety of toys you have in the house?
7. Do you allow your children to play in the street?
8. Do you allow your children to stand in a car when it is in motion or let them fiddle with the machinery?
9. Do you put a pacifier around the infant's neck?
10. Do you encourage children to play door-banging games?
11. Is the furniture in the house properly kept or does it encourage children to climb over it to look out of the window and then have nasty falls?
12. Do you keep children away when using electric wringers, mixers, sewing machine etc?
13. Do you leave the baby alone in the bath tub?
14. Have you taught the older child swimming?
15. Do you make sure that the electric appliance is unplugged when it is no longer in use?

16. Do you play with the child who is busy eating food?
17. Do you allow the child to play with a cord or string around the neck?
18. Do you destroy the discarded medicines?
19. Do you tell the child the "pill" is sweet?
20. Have you put a proper label on the kerosene oil container?

23

PLAY AND TOYS

Just the other day I met a 60-year-old who was obsessed with the notion that "play is nothing but a way of whiling away time." Of course he was not the only one holding such a view. Many people, in fact, think that play has no use.

To say the truth, play is the first work the child learns to do. Wrote Shakespeare: "Play is the superb medium to gain knowledge and learning."

It is through play that children train themselves for useful work when they grow up. Play also helps them to build a healthy physique and a sound mind. By creating several play situations, such as a train, a house or a bridge, the child develops his power of imagination and skill. All too often, the child may give you an idea through his involvement in a particular type of play whether his aptitude is for medicine, engineering or some other vocation. A friend tells me how his younger brother, now a pilot, had been highly fascinated by toy aeroplanes when he was a child.

So, don't ever discourage your son or daughter from playing. Remember, play is as much required as water, food and mothering (yes, fathering too) for a child's normal development. What is more, it helps to develop his power of patience and team spirit as well.

Types of play

Imagine a little baby fondling his mother's breasts as a toy. Soon he begins to play with his own body as well. All this gives him sensual amusement. This is what is called *sensuous play*. Not satisfied with his mother's breasts and his own body, he soon needs attractive toys to meet his increasing demand for new stimuli and fresh exploration. And, also for comfort!

Added to it in due course is the *imitative play*, which is the way the child learns the skills of being a person. By imitating speech he produces speech. He sees his parents dressing and undressing and learns these skills by imitation. Watching seniors feeding themselves, he learns to display this skill when the time comes.

What comes next is the *creative play* which means that the child creates something that, to him, was not existing earlier. Making a painting, a sketch, a model of clay or a brick building are examples of creative play.

Selecting the playthings (toys)

Mind you, while choosing toys for your child, remember that the toy is for the child and not for you or the granny. It should be durable, rich in play potential (not a showpiece to just lie there) and offer a suitable challenge to the child's ability. Also, see that the toy does not have rough, sharp edges which may cause cuts on fingers. Avoid buying toys with small detachable pieces that can be swallowed. Also, see that no poisonous material has been used on it as a paint or the like.

Needless to say, expensive toys need not be ideal for the child. I suggest simple and economic wooden or plastic blocks without any reservations. Not only does the child pick up colours, shapes and sizes through playing with these, he also gets an immense pleasure by creating such things as a house, a train, a gate or a bridge. These blocks can be used for many years. Of course, the situation he creates with advancing age bears evidence to his improving skill and imagination.

I have seen children making excellent playthings out of empty tins, clay, sand or discarded photofilm spools. Likewise a rag-doll or a puppy made at home gives the child a great deal of satisfaction.

There is no limit to the variety of toys that are available or that can be manipulated. What one needs to bear in mind is that a toy that is immensely enjoyed by a 9-month-old may not be of any use to a child of 5 years of age. The following table gives a list of suggested toys for the various age groups.

Age Group	Suggested Toys
0 to 1 year	Mobiles, Rattles, Rubber animals, Mirrors, Finger balls, Push alongs and pull alongs.
1 to 2 years	Push alongs and pull alongs, Building blocks, Shape-matching, First matching puzzles, Tunnel bricks, Scrapbooks, Picture books, Musical instruments or anything that makes noise, Slide-about car.
2 to 4 years	Dolls, Balls, Crayons, More complex puzzles, Picture dominoes.
4 to 6 years	Jigsaws, Calculating games, Puppets, Roller skates, Doctor's sets, Domestic pets, Elementary dancing, Multibuilder.

You should not hesitate to put the little one to play and at times to actually participate in it. Why not join in as much as possible when the child is pretending to ride a train or getting off it or some other such play?

Do not ever, for Heaven's sake, take away a child's favourite toy "as a part of punishment". Nothing hurts him more.

24

THE GIFTED CHILD

Every now and then our newspapers keep flashing box-items about *child prodigies*. True, children who find coverage in the mass media are with miraculous gift(s). They are eminenty exceptional. Imagine the Chinese girl who reads through her ears!

No, I do not propose to talk about a child prodigy here. What I have in mind is the frequently encountered children with relatively high potentials and special ability.

Only recently I bumped into this 8-year-old boy, Raju, in a train. Right under my nose he beat at least three experts in chess. His parents confided in me that his elder brother, aged 10, had made many champions in carrom in Baroda "keel over like a house of cards".

My own youngest brother could repair a transistor radio, like a qualified radio-engineer, when he was yet to be 10.

A 4-year-old niece of mine talks and behaves like a clever adolescent.

Yet another 10-year-old, son of a former Member of Parliament, discusses eminently politics with people 4 to 6 times his age. "Well, politics has been in our blood," his eldest sister tells me, "but, then father says that my brother has picked it up rather too fast and too early."

Identifying the gifted child

As soon as you feel that your child is specially gifted, try to look up a child psychologist. He will confirm if the child really has rich potentials. He will also guide you as to how to supply the child the much-needed additional stimulus. In the absence of such a stimulus, he is likely to get frustrated and emotionally disturbed. Rather than making use of his special ability, he may indulge in delinquency.

In order to exploit the extraordinary potentials of and to provide adequate additional stimulus to such children, the United Kingdom has an organisation ("National Association for Gifted Children") which is striving to set up special opportunity classes for them within the normal comprehensive school setting. In India, the *Child Health Study Group*, a voluntary organisation, is striving on similar lines.

His emotional needs

Just because the child is of high intellect does not mean his emotional needs can be easily ignored. Mrs. Golda Meyer is on record as saying: "I was supposed to be a super-intelligent child. Yet, what no one apparently realised, was that I needed to play with dolls. The hurt it caused continues to be fresh in my mind."

The great pianist Arturo Rubinstein tells how, when he was aged 4, he regarded his piano-playing as "like breathing" and was rather puzzled when he was widely praised for it. He goes on to tell how hurt he felt when no one praised him at all for what to him was a great achievement—being able to jump down the last two steps on the staircase.

So, parents need to remember well to satisfy all aspects of their gifted child's personality. Else, his special ability will not be fully exploited. Nothing can be sadder than that. Isn't it so?

25

THE DIFFICULT CHILD

Every now and then I, like many of my colleagues dealing with children, find myself face to face with parents who are grumbling: "Look at this nutty character, he has made our life hell. He is just a $1\frac{1}{2}$ year-old but is always on the go, creating dirty scenes everywhere. One day, Doctor, he will drive us mad."

You'll not burn your fingers if you appreciate that *negativism* is a normal trait of children between 9 months and 3 years. During this period the child wants to do just the opposite of what the mother suggests. Take it easy. He will gradually grow out of it. Any stubbornness on your part to break the child's will, may develop in him such behaviour problems as bed-wetting, temper tantrums and nail-biting.

The term *difficult* or *troublesome child* refers to such children whose upbringing in relation to parents, other family children and school is encountered with considerable difficulty.

Mismanagement by the parents tops the list of various factors that directly or indirectly lead to this problem. Such parents do not see eye to eye on child rearing with each other. The result: if the father asks the child to go to school, the mother does just the opposite, asking him to stay back with her on some flimsy pretext. Note how bad terms between the parents ruin the life of the child who in turn makes the parents' life also miserable.

Misuse of the powerful weapon of approval and disapproval can also do lots of damage to the child. As, for example, a growing child may offend his parents by his overactivity and too much of inquisitiveness. If the parents express their disapproval, the child will begin to weep as a mark of his protest to his parents' unreasonable attitude. Such a thing is bound to occur every now and then, making the child have quite a few behaviour problems.

A strong-willed child who is used to have his own way may begin to have *temper tantrums* once the parents start offering resistance to his unreasonable demands. In the commonest form of temper tantrum, he kicks and hits the chairs and the table or any other object that comes in his way. He screams louder and may throw the objects on the floor. Remember to ignore these tantrums: neither punish him nor oblige him by satisfying his unreasonable demand. That is how these are eminently managed.

Destructiveness, hitting and biting other children are all attention-seeking devices.

Lastly, to quote Professor R.S. Illingworth, "when your child is being really difficult and you are at your wits' end, try loving him more, showing how you love him more, and reprimanding less; children appreciate love more when they are being really horrid."

26

THE HANDICAPPED CHILD

Any child who demonstrates a physical, mental or psychological departure from the "normal" is a handicapped child.

Crippling of a limb or two, blindness, deafness, cleft lip or palate etc. are instances of "physical handicaps". Mental subnormality or retardation is one type of "mental handicap". Maladjustment, emotional deprivation and loss of parents will render a child "psychologically handicapped".

According to conservative estimates, India alone has about 1.5 million mentally retarded children, 3 lakh deaf, 5 lakh blind, and 4 lakh crippled children.

There is, no doubt, a clearcut place of medical or surgical treatment in handicapped children. But, its role may well be only up to a point. I have seen many parents not accepting the child's disability and then flitting from doctor to doctor and institute to institute, hoping that some miracle may happen somewhere. This is wrong and only adds to your as also to the child's problems. You should, by all means, secure the best possible treatment. But, once you know all medical opinion favours the same diagnosis and the same management, it is advisable to accept it. What is important is that both you and the child should accept the "reality" and then start endeavouring to live with it.

You can certainly assist the child to make the best use of the disability. I have seen children with nasty crippling from cerebral palsy or poliomyelitis learning to run and play games just like normal children after they are trained on artificial limbs. Many children without arms have learnt to feed themselves, to draw sketches and to write.

If they did it, why cannot others?

Speaking at a function in connection with the International Year of the

Disabled, the late Prime Minister, Mrs. Indira Gandhi said: "If cruel destiny gave them a raw deal, depriving, them of their vital limbs or the like, it is up to us to change their destiny."

True! According to *The Times of India* of June 26, 1981, a student, Bal Gilbile, of Maharashtra's Kolhapur district, who writes with his left foot, has passed the secondary school certificate examination.

Disabled since birth with no hands, the boy began practising to write with his foot and eventually mastered the art. He can also swim and ride a bicycle.

Helen Keller, though blind and deaf, has rendered excellent service to the world of writing. Toulouse Lautrec is on record to have produced outstanding art in spite of his crippling. Surdas, Milton, Edison and Homer are well known to have climbed to great heights though they were in some way or the other handicapped.

Of the living legends, can you forget the noted danseuse and actress, Sudha Chandran? She has artificial leg. Yet, her dance performance has been spectacular, moving the heart of millions the world over. She is bound to go down in the annals of history as a great dancer by virtue of her sheer dedication. Today, we hardly think of her as a disabled person. Do we?

Or, take the case of Satish Gujral who has made it big in the world of art. Do we think of him as a handicapped person? Of course, no!

Handicapped child's needs

Never forget to take care of the emotional, psychological and social aspects of the handicapped child's personality. Your attitude is going to have a lot of bearing on the performance of the child. Make sure that, as far as possible, he is treated like other children in the family. He does not need your pity. His need is to gain him independence to try and to achieve tasks graded to his ability. Of course, you and other children in the family can assist him.

Are the requirements of a handicapped child very much different from those of the normal child? No, no! The needs are more or less the same. But the problems may be complex. You require rather different ways and means to satisfy them.

Mind you, like any other child, a handicapped child is in dire need of affection and love. Unfortunately that does not always come from all parents. Many feel such a child is a sort of stigma to the family. Sometimes a sense of guilt also overwhelms them. As a result, they may reject the child though, at times, they may overprotect him. All that is rather sad.

Though a particular handicapped child may need to be placed in a special school or institute, it is generally agreed now that such children should as a rule attend ordinary schools. That gives them a feeling of belonging and sameness as normal children.

Available welfare services

In order to provide a complete package of welfare services to the handicapped individuals and groups, the following national institutions have been set up by the Government of India in each major area of disability:

(1)   National Institute for the Visually Handicapped, Dehradun, UP;
(2)   National Institute for the Orthopaedically Handicapped, Calcutta, Bengal;
(3)   Ali Yavar Jung National Institute for the Hearing Handicapped, Bombay, Maharashtra;
(4)   National Institute for the Mentally Handicapped, Hyderabad, AP;
(5)   Institute for the Physically Handicapped, New Delhi;
(6)   National Institute for Rehabilitation, Training & Research, Cuttack, Orissa.

The last two institutions have been working in the field of providing training facilities and services for rehabilitation of individuals with locomotor handicaps.

The first four institutions are national apex organisations in the field of education, vocational guidance, counselling, research, rehabilitation and development of suitable service modules for the handicapped. Besides serving as premier documentation and information centres in their respective area and imparting education, vocational training and employment, standardisation of training programmes, development of requisite manpower, development and standardisation of aids and appliances, surgical and medical procedures etc. is their responsibility.

Legislation for the handicapped

The Ministry of Welfare, Government of India, has recently set up a Committee for studying the problems faced by the handicapped persons due to non-availability of any legislation. The areas under examination of the Committee include education, employment, tax concessions, excise and custom exemption and other concessions to promote employment and rehabilitation of the handicapped.

27

SCHOOLING AND ITS PROBLEMS

Nursery school

When the child is 3 to 5 years old, it becomes increasingly difficult for the mother to keep him occupied, especially if there are no other children in the house. His need for social contacts with kids of his own age and readiness to be separated from home for some time is real and intense. It is this child who needs to be sent to nursery unless, of course, the mother is in a position to provide him happiness at home or in the closeby park or playground.

You must appreciate that, as the things exist presently in this country, nursery school is almost always the privilege of the parents who can afford to pay privately. You, perhaps, belong to that privileged class.

Remember to choose a good nursery school for your child. What you should look for is whether the building is good and well-ventilated, furniture is in good condition with chairs small enough for the children, and the teacher good-natured and receptive or not. The school should also be well-equipped with toys and playthings. Also, watch the children in the school. Do they look happy, noisy and bubbling? If the answer is yes, the school is apparently good enough for your child.

Don't simply start sending the child to nursery school. Make it a gradual process by taking him along for the first few days. The first day you should let him watch other children for half an hour. The second day make it for one hour; the third day he may like to stay back with others for a partial session. In a few days he will begin to stay there for the whole session.

Make sure that you reach the school on time to collect him after the session is over. Always. Else, he will feel deeply hurt. To him, waiting means your "indifference."

Many parents are keen to know if it is advisable to teach a nursery school-going child to read, write and do sums. The answer is: yes, it is good to expose him to the possibility of learning but never to push the things at him just because you want him to learn. If he is receptive, he will let you know. In that case you will find that he indeed enjoys early learning and new skills.

What I have recommended is the compromise answer between two schools of thought. The first pioneered by Madame Montesseri several years ago strongly advocates "early learning". The second school has such a great lot to say against urgency and anxiousness on the parents' part to overburden the child too early with learning.

The regular school

Once the child is 5 or 6 years of age, it is time to start regular school which imparts regular formal education. Choose a good school with fine reputation, a nice well-equipped building, a spacious playground and good staff. What is most important is that its students should be disciplined and happy.

Early preparation during the preceding two years of school entry will help a great lot to prevent those tearful scenes at the school gate that first morning. A child who has been trained in independence, can put on and do up his shoes, dress unaided and manipulate buttons of his trousers when he goes to the toilet, is most likely to be comfortable at school. Needless to say, the child who had been to nursery school should have no problems in the full-time school.

Remember, the success or failure of the child at school will largely depend on your own attitudes. If the mother believes school is not so important, she is likely to hold back the child at home on flimsy grounds, such as minor illness or to give her company. This is a leading cause of *school absence*. Regretfully the cause lies in parents' negative attitude to schooling.

You must remain in touch with the child's teacher(s) to find if he is doing well or not. It is good to attend parent-teacher meetings once a term. To say that these are just a "waste of time" is far from being true.

Many parents are in the habit of talking ill about the child's teacher in his presence. That is a very bad practice. It shakes the child's faith in the teacher's authority and adversely effects his learning from her. If you really are not in agreement with the teacher's assessment of the child's performance or with her ways, it is in order to have a face-to-face talk with her in the child's absence. If you find her unreasonable, talk it over with the principal of the school without causing any bitterness. In no case let the teacher feel that you do not have respect for her.

There is quite a lot of virtue in spending sometime with the child at home and assist him to sort out his difficulties in studies. It is, however, unwise to make it a prestige issue and do the homework yourself on the child's behalf simply to impress the teacher. Your job is to guide the child and not to get into the role that is essentially his. After all, it is he who is to eventually write the examination.

Lastly, always cooperate in proper conduction of the periodical medical check-up at the school. It has its distinct advantages. Not just that! Make sure the child's vaccination is uptodate several weeks before he begins going to school. In fact it is a healthy practice to have the child's complete medical check-up before starting school. Make a list of any emotional or physical problems your child has and any medication he is taking. The teacher may need information concerning family background that could have a bearing on the child's behaviour and attitudes. A small supply of drugs for emergencies such as an attack of asthma or epilepsy may be left with the teacher or the school health clinic.

As a postscript, let me impress upon you to provide your telephone numbers and those of a neighbour or a relative so that the school can contact you in case of an emergency. Also, make sure to label the school bag with your child's name, address and telephone numbers. Also, do label all contents, more so the lunch box, pencil case etc. And, make sure, the child does not take costly toys to school as many a fight in the school is over treasured toys.

Problems at school

Most children do have some difficulty or problem at school. As and when you get an inkling, join with the teacher to get an answer.

Stealing, an expression of insecurity, afflicts children whose home is lacking in love and attention.

Bullying may result from personal insecurity and inadequacy, boredom from unrecognised gift or inability to cope with the target set for him.

The solution lies not in punishing the child but in seeking the cause and remedying it.

Also, remember, if one child is bullying in the school, there may be several who are being *bullied*. A child who is bullied is usually an only child in the family. He is lacking in self-confidence, has not learnt to give and take at home, is timid, either a "fattie" or "far too thin", shows mannerism and is clumsy. The solution lies in helping the child to find his own answer to the problem. Encouraging him to take to sports usually helps considerably in tackling this rather common problem at school.

Lying is usually an expression of too little appreciation at home or in school. To impress the parents, the child may tell them, "I have topped in the test" or "I scored a century in the cricket match." At school, he takes pride in telling the teacher and the classmates that his parents are rich and that his relatives are big shots in politics or industry.

Fear of punishment also inspires the child to indulge in lying. If he has not done his homework, he might tell the teacher that his mother suddenly fell sick which she didn't.

Drug abuse and *smoking* are indulged in by some senior schoolboys and girls. The underlying factors include frustration in studies. It could be bad company, "just for kicks", out of curiosity, "to hit back at the parents and teachers" and the like.

Poor showing at school may be secondary to low intelligence, laziness, frequent absence from school, frequent changes of school, difficulties with certain subjects, wrong choice of subjects, insecurity, emotional distress etc. At times, it may be secondary to visual defects, poor hearing or general ill-health. Not uncommonly, the poor standard of teaching in the class may be the major contributing factor.

Sex play in the form of homosexuality and masturbation are all too often practised, especially in the boarding schools. These are harmless and best ignored.

School phobia, in which the child is afraid of going to school, may cause such manifestations as tummy ache, diarrhoea, vomiting,—all disappearing after school hours—loss of appetite, sleeplessness, nightmares and so on.

More often than not, the problem of school phobia is secondary to unhappiness at home.

If school phobia in the child is profound and its solution beyond your apparent control, you should approach a Child Guidance Clinic for help.

Parent-school organisation

If as a mother you have the time and energy and often feel bored and isolated at home, why not get inolved in a parent-school organisation? Hopefully, your child's school is having one.

This will help you make friends out of other parents, providing you a lot of opportunity to get to know the community. This will give extra opportunity to your child to have more and more of playmates and friends.

The choice, of course, is entirely yours. No school will ever force it on you.

28
SEX EDUCATION

Talking about sex has long been regarded as a sort of "taboo" in India. Children are thus left with no alternative but to learn about it, more often than not, in an unhealthy way. As the celebrated authority Kinsley puts it: "When parents sit on the information that they should pass on to the child, the poor child starts wondering what is so secretive about it. His curiosity and interest are further increased. He begins either to think there is something shameful about his own body or he goes out to find the answers from friends.... The eventual result in either case is usually bad."

That is why sex education is very essential. You must educate him about the biological facts tactfully.

To begin with the child should be able to see that his parents share "love" and care for each other's happiness. There is no virtue in hiding physical caressing and your bodies from the child. I am not suggesting that you should exhibit with pride your "love-making" or your stark naked bodies before the child. The point I wish to make is a little different. If the child moves in while you are kissing or caressing or dressing, or undressing, or bathing, it will be unwise to shout at him. If you do that, the child will get the impression that something bad is being hidden from him. This may be the beginning of varied sexual problems that may make his life miserable when he grows up as an adult.

As teaching parents you are expected to have full understanding of these facts. Your relaxed happy sex attitude will prove ornamental to enable you to answer your child's countless questions.

At about 2 to 4 years he may like to know why he is so different from his sister. Why does he have "something" that she does not and vice versa? Do not beat about the bush. Give him frank answers.

Where did he come from? Many parents and grandparents find it awfully difficult to talk about the process of reproduction. They try to put off the child by answering that "you were found in the store", "God sent you in a sack" or "we brought you from the temple." That is a sheer wrong way of dealing with his sensible question. Be frank and tell the child that he grew in mummy's tummy for nine months. There is nothing wrong in telling him something about how it all started in the tummy and that it was the result of strong love between the parents. You may tell the child that, when he grows up into an adult, he will get married to a cute girl. The two of them will be able to have a child or two the "same way as we had". While telling the child all this, be relaxed. Tenseness and sentimentalism will merely spoil all your talking, leaving little positive impact on the child.

Remember not to be panicky if you find the child fiddling and playing with his genitalia. That is perfectly normal. Resentment will only aggravate the things, setting a vicious circle which you will find very tough to break. Allow him to grow out of it on his own.

As the child approaches puberty, tell him he may have seminal discharge some night and that it is a normal biological phenomenon which need not worry him. The girls should likewise be told that a vaginal blood discharge is round the corner and that it will continue as a monthly feature for many years to come.

Your objective is to teach the child the facts he wants to know and the facts he needs to know so that he emerges from adolescence believing that sex and love go hand in hand. This, as Kinsley says, will equip them better to meet the stresses and strains of life when they are adults.

29
DISCIPLINE

"Foundation of good emotional health lies in love and independence"-
this is how I had concluded my article on bringing up happier children in
the *Illustrated Weekly of India* over a decade ago. One particular letter in
the overwhelming response to the article is still fresh in my mind. The
respondent, a retired professor of psychology who wanted to remain
anonymous, wrote: "Admittedly, you're right but only up to a point ....
Don't ever forget love and independence mean only half of the story. The
other half is knowing that the third basic need of the child for good
emotional health is discipline."

Needless to say, I could not join issue with the learned professor. All
these years, more so after the arrival of our own children, this has been
brought home to me time and again that children decidedly need
discipline. Early this year, I, along with my daughter and son, visited the
Kumars whose children are known to run the house, having never been
exposed to discipline. Within a matter of two hours, our children became
eager to return home having had enough of the disorderly environment.
"For a while, it was quite a fun," said my daughther, aged 7, adding, "but
all too soon, it was all chaos." So, you can see that even young children
like "order".

Discipline and punishment are not synonymous

What is discipline after all? *The Oxford Dictionary* defines it as training,
especially of the mind and character, to produce self-control, order,
obedience and the like. In the case of a child, it means that he has to learn
to conform to the set rules, behave in an acceptable manner, respect limits
of freedom rather than have his way day in and day out, and to obey the
parents etc. It is an action directed towards improving an individual. By
no means is it synonymous with punishment which implies a reaction
towards an individual—a sort of "hurt"—for his having committed a

"wrong". If you train a four-year-old not to take shoes on to the bed, you are inculcating discipline in him. On the other hand, if you give him a slap for having not obeyed your order, you are giving him a punishment.

Why discipline?

You may well ask: Why does the child need to be disciplined?

To start with, let us see what can happen if there is a lack of discipline. The child lacks manners, wrecks furniture, ruins carpets and spoils the walls and books with scratches and pencil marks. He frequently throws tantrums and is likely to be avoided by the neighbours, branded as "spoiled" or "horror".

There is ample evidence that parents of such children either had never been exposed to discipline when they were children, or they are obsessed by the notion that discipline causes repression.

Overdiscipline spoils

Don't be carried away with the impression that only lack of discipline harms the child. Much-too-much or wrong discipline may be equally harmful, causing a sense of insecurity in the child. Some children subjected to overdiscipline manifest shyness, timidity, oversubmissiveness etc. In the majority, response is just the opposite of what the parents expect from them, a sort of deliberate disobedience. They appear not to be hearing the instructions. Such manifestations as negativism, aggressiveness, rebellion and temper tantrums may occur.

What kind of parents indulge in overdiscipline? First, those who have no idea as to what type of discipline is to be expected from a child of a particular developmental age. Take the case of Sabharwals who once spoke to me about their 2-year-old daughter who was so averse to their constant pressure on her to wash her hands before she chose to eat something. I simply wondered at the undue expectations of the parents. A girl of 2 years of age is simply not old enough to learn such rigid disciplinary command. At the age of 3, she can certainly learn it.

The second kind of parents indulging in excessive discipline are those who boss over their children to satisfy their ego, as an outlet for their hurt, sense of dignity, to make up for the loss of face or as a habit to force everything on the child, including food, sleep, bowel movement and obedience. Imagine a young woman causing a nasty scene in my clinic just because her daughter, aged 4, chose to fondle my stethoscope. Not because it was desirable but only because she wanted to make a demonstration of the child's instant obedience. In the process, all she attained was an exposure of her own hollowness.

I can recall another woman. Everytime I saw her, she was constantly nagging her 10-year-old son. "No, Aditya no, this is bad", "O, no, don't be a bad boy", "No, why don't you sit properly?" and the like were her common sayings. Did the child become well-behaved, well-mannered, obedient and highly disciplined? No, far from that. What he became was a staunch rebel and often met with some accident.

Before it slips my mind, let me impress upon you that erratic discipline—never mind it is "under" or "over" — is a known cause of accident proneness. In a recent study, Dr. Annie Jullie and Dr. Anil Bhaskar found that in 88 per cent of the children with accidents, the parents had either given the child overpermissiveness (lack of discipline) or they were overindulgent in enforcing excessive discipline.

All said and done, the crux of the whole discussion is that balanced discipline taught with firmness and loving tolerance is an essential emotional need of the growing child. A child exposed to such discipline comes up happier and healthier. He, when the time comes in later years, is capable of exerting self-discipline.

Fundamental principles

Let us see what the fundamental principles about imparting discipline are:

1. First, *pay due respect to the child's level of learning skills*. Though teaching of discipline may be started somewhere between 1 and 3 years, you must remember that a child of 1 year is unlikely to learn discipline whereas he can learn it at the age of 3. Rather than the chronological age, it is the mental age that is more important. A mentally subnormal child even at the age of 4 years may not be ready to be disciplined since his chronological age may be just 2 years. Hence, attempts on the part of the parents to force discipline on him may lead to problems that only backfire rather than benefit the child and the parents.

2. Second, *win the child's confidence, establishing yourself as an authority that needs to be obeyed*. The spoken command meant for compliance needs to be reinforced with physical enforcement without giving much of reasoning and, of course, nagging, scolding or punishment. A 3-year-old needs to be summoned for lunch as you hold his hand and guide him to the dining room. Explanations in the case of young children lead nowhere.

3.   Third, *make only few time-tested rules and ensure their compliance.* It is of no use to enforce discipline of the kind that is impractical. Thus, there is no wisdom in such instructions as "You must sleep now", "You must eat your food", or "Stop crying".

4.   Fourth, *practise consistency.* Mrs. Ameeta Khanna would forbid her 8-year-old son, Sonu, to roll down the railing but condone the same act at times, depending on her mood rather than any rationale. Understandably, this left the child utterly confused. So, ensure that discipline is consistent as far as workable. Small wonder that little breaches must be ignored.

5.   Fifth, *establish agreement on modes of disciplining.* It badly confuses the child if the mother forbids him to do a particular thing but the father or the grandparents simply condone the act. Eventually, he says, "To hell with it" and refuses to listen to any advice or teaching concerning discipline.

6.   Sixth, *inculcate discipline with firmness, love, tolerance, praise and reward rather than threats of punishment, actual punishment or criticism.* The parents must discipline the child through love, respect and example set by them. Scolding and punishment are the thing of the past and are best left alone. As Professor R.S. Illingworth puts it, "the child should behave well because he wants to do, because he wants the approval of the parents whom he loves, and because he wants the approval of the teachers."

And, some don'ts

You as parents must learn to criticise the act and not the child. Tell him "Spitting is bad and you must not do it", and not "You're a bad boy as you spit..." In the second expression which I have chosen to condemn, there is an assault on the child's self-esteem. Such an attack hurts most and can prove dangerous to the child's psyche and further relationship between the parents and the child.

Remember to discipline the child through reward, never bribery. The latter gives the child the option of choosing and can be destructive.

You should always give the child an opportunity to explain whether the wrong he did was deliberate or a sheer accident. A certain mother was in the habit of firing, "Idiot, don't answer back and argue.... A little utterance from you and I'll smash your head." Result: destructiveness.

"Threats" of punishment are decidedly wrong. All that the parents achieve through this means is that the child gets frightened (some call it "submissiveness", is it so?). An IAS friend's spouse threatens her children virtually all the time in terms such as this: "Repeat that nonsense just once more and see how I handle you." My suggestion is that if you strongly feel the child does need a light punishment, give it then and there. The whole thing should be spontaneous.

While I am still talking about threats, never use "dad" as a threat, saying things like: "Let your father return home. You'll be in for hell." Why can't the mother have the rules of behaviour? And, God, why can't she see to it that these are honoured, irrespective of whether the father is at home or away.

Another piece of suggestion: Don't, for God's sake, ever say that if the child does a mischief, you won't love him. Remember, the greatest terror a child can have is to be told by the parents that he is or he won't be loved any more.

And, yet one more: One thing you must avoid is overdo the loss of pocket money or privileges to discipline him the way you want. This kind of unfairness confuses him and he seldom forgets it. Result: unhealthy parent-child relationship and conflict.

Finally, let me conclude, dear readers, by saying that if you do all this, you shouldn't have much "bother" with the problem of discipline.

30

BEHAVIOUR PROBLEMS

1. Years ago, when I was working on a study on behaviour problems, an agitated young couple approached me about their 5-year-old son, Bunty, who not only indulged in nail-biting and thumb-sucking but also in bed-wetting during sleep. The mother said, "Every now and then I have to thrash him right and left but the things are rather worsening."

2. Sonu, a 3-year-old, would eat such non-edible stuffs as crayons, worn-out paint, dirt or paper. An old lady next door had advised the parents to "lock her in a dark room if she does the silly thing again". The result: the child cried and cried, and became blue and limp, sending shock waves all around. The doctor attending on her diagnosed the problem as breath-holding spell. In the months to follow, even minor argumentation would lead to temper tantrums and such spells.

3. A child of 5, Chintu, was brought by his worried mother for stammering, shyness, night terrors and refusal to eat. She remarked in the child's very presence that "this congenital idiot will someday drive me mad." Then, and only then, the son and the father would learn a lesson, added she.

4. Ritu, 8, was said to be getting on the nerves of her parents for her abusive language, lying and stealing. All attempts to thrash her into obedience and decent behaviour had only backfired. What was worse, according to the father, she was beginning to be destructive as well.

5. In the case of 6-year-old Raju, the problem was absolute refusal to go to school. While the overindulgent mother narrated the details of the problem, the father appeared to be simply disinterested.

Such stories of behaviour difficulties could be duplicated, nay multiplied, by those involved in child care. It is unusual to have a behaviour difficulty in isolation. If there is one behaviour problem, there is more often than not another. In our own experience, around 10 per cent of the children attending the outpatient department of the Government Children Hospital suffer from behaviour problems. What is noteworthy is the observation that almost 80 per cent of the sufferers have more than one behaviour difficulty.

What is a behaviour problem?

You may well ask what a behaviour problem is after all. This, remember, is a child's way of reacting to a difficult environmental situation—a sort of cry for help. You may regard it as a deviation of normal behaviour to a point at which remedial action is not all that simple and effective.

Mind you, the dividing line between normal and abnormal behaviour is not quite clearcut. It fluctuates with age, social settings, and cultural background. Not just that. In the same individual, it may vary from time to time depending on the intensity and effect of stress which is now considered essential to cause abnormal behaviour in an essentially normal child.

Behaviour Problems at a Glance

Habit Problems
Thumb-sucking, nail-biting, tics, enuresis (bed-wetting)

Eating Problems
Pica, food refusal, vomiting, food fads

Sleep Problems
Night terrors, nightmares, sleep-walking, sleep-talking

Speech Problems
Stammering, stuttering

Personality Problems
Jealousy, shyness, timidity, fears, bouts of anger

Scholastic Problems
Reading, writing or mathematical disability, school phobia, absenteeism, repeated failures, aggressiveness

Sexual Problems
Masturbation, homosexuality

Antisocial Problems
Juvenile delinquency in the form of stealing, lying, destructiveness, gang activities

And, its basis?

Why does the child indulge in an odd behaviour? To quote Freud, odd behaviour is a reaction to a wide variety of factors operating before pregnancy, during pregnancy, during delivery, in neonatal period, and in subsequent environments from time to time.

Let me make it clear that by environment is meant what we doctors label as "emotional environment". This relates to such factors as parental attitudes, siblings, neighbourhood, school and mass media including movies, television, radio and magazines etc.

The faulty parental attitudes are the single most important cause of behaviour difficulties, especially in a young child. Emotional conflicts resulting from such attitudes may be related to either overprotection or rejection.

Overprotection means more than excessive protection of the child against danger with the result that he is not allowed to take care of himself and grow up like his peers who are given balanced protection. I know of one Mrs. Uma Chopra who considered her little daughter "far too delicate" and the "only link with her late husband" who had been killed in an air-crash. The lady never allowed the daughter to go out on her own lest she caught a cold or mixed with rough children and learnt bad language. Even her homework was more or less done by the overindulgent mother. Overconscious of child's health, she was virtually daily recording her body temperature with an "imported" thermometer and getting her stools tested every week. Result: the girl turned out to be overdependent and was late in picking up various skills. Not just that. She turned out to be immature, timid, friendless and vulnerable to bullying at school. Now an adolescent, she is beginning to develop manifestations of aggressive behaviour.

Overprotection may happen in the only child, the only son, a child born after many years of waiting, the first son (more so when this is a joint family), a very goodlooking child, a mentally or physically-handicapped child, in case of loss of a spouse or failure on the part of a spouse to play his or her role well, or a child who is supposed to have brought fortune to the parents etc.

Rejection, on the other hand, usually accompanied by favouritism to the other child, may amount to failure to attend to the normal needs of the child, unfavourable comparisons, sending to an institution when the circumstances do not demand it, unnecessary scolding, excessive punishment, or failure to please the child consistently with a reward as and when appropriate.

Rejection, as you would appreciate, may happen in an unwanted child, an illegitimate child, a step-child, a mentally or physically-handicapped child, a child who is supposed to have brought bad luck to the family, or a child who is chronically mischievous and a constant source of troubles for the parents.

Interestingly enough, quite often the faulty parental attitudes may well be a mixture of overprotection at one time and rejection at another, depending on such diverse factors as parents' mood, financial position, job-satisfaction, interparental relationship etc. Lack of consistency on the part of the parents confuses the child, leading to conflict, anxiety and insecurity.

You can, therefore, see that the cause of disturbed behaviour in a large majority of the children is insecurity, tension or lack of love. Nevertheless, do not walk off with the impression that I am trying to blame the parents and raising an accusing finger. Far from that! Parents, in fact, have their own personality problems which need attention. What they learn from friends, doctors, books and magazines often gives them conflicting advice. Consequent upon that, they are at their wits' end as to what to do.

The way out

The question arises: What, then is the way out? My earnest suggestion is that you turn to your family doctor for help for the behaviour problems of your child. Of course, you should do that after making a thorough search for the cause at your own level with an unbiased mind. An interested doctor can be of immense help to you and your child. He will make you see the real nature of the difficulty and isolate the factors in the emotional environment that caused intense anxiety. He will also assist you to cope with the situation and, possibly, remove the offending causative factor(s).

No wonder, most qualified child specialists manage many more children with behaviour disturbances than is usually realised. Knowing the family well puts the doctor in an advantageous position to recall the attitudes that may be contributing to child's emotional problems.

I must emphasize the usefulness and value of free and frank projection of the child's as well as your own problems to the doctor. The other day, I heard a yound lady, who had just been to the family physician, making this silly statement: "I wonder why the hell he was interested in our attitudes and personal problems. All I wanted him to do was solve the problem of delinquency in our son."

You can appreciate how such a consultation from the physician proves of little or no worth. Just because the lady had no idea that the child's problems are not to be seen in isolation! The physician must be given the chance to understand the family and the rest of the child's environment. How else can he do his job well?

Remember, it is not enough for the physician to know only one parent since both parents influence the child's behaviour—not only by their direct relationship with him but also by their influence on one another.

And, before I forget, make a note that there are other relationships of importance (including siblings, peers, grandparents, uncles, aunts, cousins, teachers and students in the school) that may also need to be looked into in evaluating the child's odd behaviour. So, be ready to help the physician on this front as well.

More often than not, the educated folks are given to understand that all behaviour problems need a specialist's advice. That is just not true. So, don't be overzealous in rushing for such a consultation.

Undoubtedly, as and when your doctor feels that a consultation from a psychologist or a psychiatrist is indicated, he will certainly advice you to seek it.

31

THE STORMY TEENS

1. According to a middle-aged lady, "We are quite upset that our 12-year old son, Sonu has just begun to neglect his studies. He is preoccupied with his own self." On the contrary, she said, the 10 year-old daughter, who had a reputation for being slack at school, had developed a renewed interest in scholastic work.

2. A 10-year-old convent-going boy, who is perhaps one of the very few boys in his class, is distressed that most of the girls in the class have recently grown much taller than him. "Man, some of them really look matured and dignified," he says. "I am yet to mature like that." He wonders if "I am an underdeveloped pig."

3. The parents of a 15-year-old tell me, "He has lost direction. He picks fights with us over trifles. He is beginning to revolt." He retaliates in still stronger words. To quote him, "What revolt? I am no longer a child. I too need freedom. What is there if I court a girl friend? I demand my rights and dignities. How long will my dad and mummy deny me all that?"

4. A girl who had not been warned about "menstruation" wrote this note to a confidante the day she had her first period: "I am terribly scared. I do not know what wrong I have done to deserve this fate. I cannot even talk to my parents about it. What'll they think?"

These instances have been specially picked to focus attention on some of the highlights of the stormy period of transition, the so-called *adolescence*. As has been rightly put, "Adolescence is much more than one rung up the ladder from childhood. It is a built-in, necessary transition period for ego development. It is a leave-taking of the dependencies of childhood and precocious reach for adulthood. An adolescent is a traveller who has left one place and has not reached the next.... It is an intermission between earlier freedoms... and subsequent responsibilities and commitments... a last hesitation before... serious commitments concerning work and love."

Adolescence and puberty

What is the precise adolescence period? It is difficult to define it. But, broadly speaking, adolescence starts when the individual attains sexual maturity and ends when independence from parental authority is assured. Since the age of sexual maturing varies a lot, marking off the beginning of adolescence is rather difficult.

Are adolescence and puberty synonymous? No, not really. Whereas adolescence refers to all stages of maturing, puberty relates to sexual maturing only.

Adolescence, for instance, extends from 13 to 18 years in girls and 14 to 18 years in boys. Puberty, on the contrary, is an overlapping period. Out of an average of 4 years, about 2 years are spent in preparing for the body reproduction (this period overlaps the end of childhood, the so-called *pre-adolescence* and *pubescence*). The remaining 2 years are spent in completing the process; these overlap early adolescence.

On an average, *growth spurt* occurs at 10 to 12 years in girls and 12 to 13 years in boys. The child shows remarkable gain in height in a year. Since girls usually have spurt earlier than the boys by about two years, girls of the same age as that of the boys will be taller, more mature and more sophisticated than the boys. All too soon (in a couple of years or so), the boys, however, do catch up.

The control of puberty is by the *endocrine glands* which are found in the brain (pituitary glands), in the neck (thyroid glands); on top of the kidneys (adrenal glands) and reproductive system (testicles in males, ovaries in females). These glands produce chemical substances known as *hormones.*

Puberty changes in girls

Puberty changes in girls begin to show up at 10 to 12 years. Their common order of appearance is:

(i) Breast changes, like pigmentation of areola and enlargement of breast tissue and nipple, are perhaps the earliest to occur. In a good proportion of the girls, one breast grows faster than the other. The girl is likely to feel distressed over this odd development. She needs to be reassured that, with passage of time, the size dissimilarity would disappear.

Most growing girls are under the impression that their nipples should always remain erect and tight. That is not true.

Some girls have inverted nipples or non-protruding nipples. This again is no issue for worrying. The mother should feel convinced that all is well and tell the same to the growing girl in no uncertain terms. In the event of the problem still causing undue anxiety to the girl, it would be in order to seek medical opinion.

(ii) Increase in pelvic girth and the resultant broadening of the hips.

(iii) Appearance of pubic hair. Hair may also appear on other body parts including armpits.

(iv) Menarche, i.e. the first menstruation or bleed occurs usually 2 years after first manifestation of puberty. It is held that menstruation generally occurs every 28 days and lasts for 5 days on an average.

Every mother needs to tell her adolescent daughter that, in puberty in particular, periods may occur at 3 weeks, 6 weeks or longer intervals. Also, the period may vary from 2 days to 7 days; so may happen with the intensity of blood loss: it may be scanty or heavy.

A year after the onset of menarche, the girl is likely to establish a more or less definite menstrual cycle of her own which would persist in later years.

The mother should guide her adolescent daughter about the use of a readymade sanitary napkin (disposable is to be preferred) that she can wear with comfort and confidence.

What is also to be remembered is that a high strung personality, illness or anxiety may lead to a very heavy blood loss or to skipping of the period.

There are girls in whom lower abdominal cramps—at times almost disabling—accompany the period. Yet, another group of teenagers suffer from tender and swollen breasts a little before or during the period. Such girls need reassurance and normal activity. Anti-pain tablets often prove handy to them.

Though girls should regard menstruation as a normal physiological function like passing urine or motion, quite often it is the other way round. Many girls are unfortunately conditioned to expect that they would "suffer as badly" as their fussy mothers do during the menstrual period. When their time comes, they behave "just as the mother does" with painful menstruation and anxiety. This is called *dysmenorrhoea*. The latter could well be the result of a medical problem—the unevenness of hormone production. So, remember to consult the doctor as and when in doubt.

Puberty changes in boys

It is around the age of 12 to 13 years that puberty changes in boys start appearing. The sequence of events is as follows:

(i) Enlargement of external genitals i.e., penis and testicles.

(ii) Appearance of pubic hair followed by hair in armpits, groin, thighs and between pubis and umblicus (navel). Facial hair appears about 2 years after the pubic hair.

(iii) Changes in voice. The voice breaks and is odd. It fits neither with that of the child nor the adult.

(iv) Nocturnal discharge of semen involuntarily, often as the adolescent is asleep during night, is as important to a boy as menstruation to a girl. It is also popularly referred to as *wet dream*. The parents must communicate to him that it is a perfectly normal phenomenon and is in fact a sign of his "manliness". Else, he may suffer from a feeling of guilt and anxiety.

Recently I asked 100 successive fathers of teenage boys: "Did you ever forewarn your child about the first ejaculation of seminal fluid and the so-called *wet dreams*? Did you tell him all that was perfectly normal and needed to cause no worry?" Just imagine only 10 gentlemen replied in affirmative to my first question. There was only one "yes" to the second query.

The mothers would do well to remember that they must see to it that the father does find time to guide their growing child on this score. Else, the child's guilt has already done him a grave harm before he learns from somewhere that "it is all normal and harmless."

Adolescent and sex

The importance of sex drive in adolescent behaviour is vital. Freud has gone a step further in saying that "sexuality affects and is affected" by behaviour in every sphere of life and activity. Imagine when he stresses that "sex drive is the basis for all constructive action"which, perhaps, will not be agreed upon by some!

It is important to appreciate that a girl is capable of becoming a mother as soon as she starts her menstruation. In the same way, a boy can become a father once he begins to have ejaculation of seminal fluid containing sperms produced by the testicles. Yet, remember they are not capable of parental responsibility at this early stage. They need to be told that teens should be crossed before they embark on ultimate sexual adventure. That is not to say that intermixing with the opposite sex should be discouraged. On the contrary, it should be encouraged. What is significant is that the parents must speak to their teenagers in a spirit of love and understanding, clarifying the difference between "healthy and mature friendliness" and "practical sex adventure." "Love" must take decided priority over "sexuality" during adolescence.

Masturbation: Almost every teenager—yes, boys as well as girls—find pleasant sensation by handling the external genitals and achieving what is known as *orgasm*.

The so-called, *self-gratification, self-stimulation* or *masturbation* is, in a way, the adolescent's attempt to kick out the "sex fire" smouldering inside the body. It does give him comfort.

Many children demonstrate rhythmic fondling of the genitals as early as the third year of life. But it is only at puberty that a boy will get *erection* as well as discharge of semen. The boys achieve orgasm by rubbing the penis against something (may be a cushion, quilt or dummy) or by handling the organ in their hands. What they try to accomplish is a mimicry of the act of intercourse through thrusting movements.

What are the exciting factors which lead to the erection of the penis? Sex fantasies, sex discussion, reading about sex stories, "sexciting" pictures of girls, sexy movies, or as simple a thing as friction may act as a "stimulus". The "stimulus" fills the sponge-like penis with lots of warm blood. As a result the organ changes into a stiff, erect and strong structure whose size will vary from person to person.

The frequency of masturbation varies from individual to individual. Some do it just once in a while whereas others may masturbate quite a few times everyday. Researchers say that 99 per cent of the men and women have indulged in this practice at one time or another.

Is masturbation harmful? No. In fact it is an absolutely normal behaviour. It is a natural thing to do. Many authorities describe it as an "essential component of an adolescent's psycho-sexual development."

The parents must realise this fact and tell the teenager son or daughter so in clearcut terms.

Many parents, on the other hand, mishandle the situation. It is absurd to get into the teenager's head that masturbation is "bad", "a wicked thing to do", or "a dirty, stupid habit". There are parents who tell their sons that "if you repeat the silly thing, you will become impotent" or "you do it again and your penis will surely fall." Such parents hardly understand that threats like that are very damaging to the boy.

Masturbation is more or less a harmless thing and the parents are advised to ignore it rather than to make it an issue. Else, the sense of "guilt" will tear the teenager inside out and upside down. Serious anxiety and fear tells upon his personality a great deal. He gradually withdraws from his social circle and becomes self-centred. His school work suffers as also his performance in the playground. But, does all that stop the habit? Hardly! As a matter of fact, it establishes its roots still more. It is a different matter that he may make sure that parents do not get an inkling of his "doing".

So, parents, don't be fussy and anxious if your son or daughter indulges in "self-gratification". Even at the expense of repetition, I must say that it is just a harmless habit, leading to neither impotency nor insanity, epilepsy, brain damage, growth failure or anything else. If your ward is doing much-too-much of it, divert his attention to swimming, sports or some other interest that he finds appealing. But do not ever cause a feeling of "guilt" in the little man or woman. Please... please! Else, you would find yourself backfired.

Homosexuality: In families where interest in sex is regarded "taboo" and repressed, child-parent relationship is unhealthy and children are made to live unhappily. Odd sex problems often result among the adolescents. *Homosexuality* refers to sexual involvement of an individual with a member of the same sex rather than that of the opposite sex.

Eminent researchers believe that, more often than not, roots of homosexuality are laid in childhood *per se*. As for instance, dressing a girl in boy's clothing or the boy in that of the girl may have far-reaching repercussions. Some parents pride in scolding children for evincing interest in the opposite sex and in censoring the movies they see, books they read or the exhibitions they visit. It has been found that in a majority of the cases of homosexuality the father is of a weak personality whereas the mother is dominant and overprotective.

Where do we go from here? It is felt that the problem of homosexuality can be adequately dealt with if parents exercise caution and understanding in handling children. They should not discourage children from getting answers to their queries about sex. Neither should they project sex interest as "silly" or "disgraceful". Also, it is a healthy practice to put the children in co-educational schools rather than institutions where sexes are segregated.

It is a common observation that in a vast majority of the homosexual boys and girls the habit dies down before long. The parents should not pay much attention to the "perversion". Too much fussiness and anxiety will only aggravate it. An explanation of the sexual role and its ultimate objective and understanding on the part of the teenager as he matures will finally induce his interest in the opposite sex.

Venereal diseases: As I said earlier a teenager is capable of producing children but is, however, not suited to do so at this stage. He should, therefore, refrain from rushing into an actual sex encounter. You, perhaps, are given to understand that all the teenagers do, in fact, avoid the "forbidden apple". They don't. That's pity, however.

Experience has shown that the incidence of teenage mothers and fathers is constantly increasing, not only in the permissive society of the West but also among the Asians.

Also, venereal diseases (syphilis and gonorrhoea) in the very young are now seen in rising rates. One cause of this rise is increasing curiosity on the part of the adolescent to explore the *Pandora's box* since he has seldom been explained the mystery of sex. Another factor that has contributed to it is the overemphasis on sex and permissiveness in the movies and commercial advertisements and the so-called *blue films* which have now invaded India and other Asian countries in a big way.

The parents and the teachers will do well to ensure that the young receive sex education to prevent such avoidable disease and trauma. They should resolve the youngsters' doubts in open discussions. The time and energy devoted on sermons about chastity, if diverted to practical sex education, would bring gratifying and fruitful dividends.

The problem of drug abuse

Drug habit it no longer a rarity among the adolescents in the Asian countries. All-India surveys indicate as high an incidence as 3 per cent of *addiction* and 15 per cent of *casual indulgence* among senior school-going boys and girls. The prevalence is particularly high in hostelers of public schools.

Drugs generally abused are sleeping pills, tranquillisers, stimulants, mood-elevators, cannabis (bhang, charas, ganja) and opiates. LSD, cocaine and heroin are used by a small proportion of abusers. The majority use more than one drug.

Most of the drug addict teenagers show significant evidence of conflict, confusion, mental tension and remarkable deterioration in scholastic performance. Shoplifting, stealing and, at times, even trafficking are resorted to by the "die-hard" addicts to make enough money to procure the supply of drugs.

Why drugs? The causes include frustration at home, poor performance at school, bad company, emotional stress and the like. "Keenness to burn the midnight oil" at the time of examination and to "gear up stamina" for better performance in sports and athletics are said to be the underlying factors in some cases. Others indulge in the world of drugs "just for kicks", "just for the heck of it", "simply to see what will happen" or as an "adventure". Yet another group of adolescents consume drugs to "hit back" at the parents, teachers or society. What a protest!

To check the malady, the following measures are suggested:

(i) Provision of adequate facilities for recreation and entertainment in the families as well as in the hostels.

(ii) Proper channelisation of energies of the young people into constructive activities and other healthy interests.

(iii) Inculcation of dangers of drug abuse among adolescents. This cannot be done unless parents and teachers are aware of these dangers and take pains to educate the youngsters.

(iv) Provision of periodical psychiatric guidance facilities in schools.

(v) Strict implementation of drug control measures.

Remember, all this is a tough task. The parents have double responsibility here. In the first place they must handle the problem of drug abuse at home tactfully. Secondly, they must contribute to the implementation of the suggested measures in collaboration with other agencies. Unfortunately most parents take the problem of drug abuse very lightly. One of the investigators of the surveys (referred to a short while ago) has an interesting story to tell. In his words, "just about 6 per cent of the mothers and 5 per cent of the fathers of drug abusers contacted by us felt that they could do something to contain the malady. The rest of them simply laughed away the question." I am told that "most of them were far too busy to find time."

That is the tragedy of today's rat-race! If the parents are not eager to get out of the "rut" of their own making, how would the teenagers?

Teenager's calf love

"Look at these schoolboys and girls talking of love affairs," is what a middle-aged lady fired at a party. A host of women joined her. Said one, "Boy friend! Girl friend! That is what they have been talking about at this young age. Funny!" Added another, "Heavens, today's teenagers are going to the dogs. They care for nothing and boss over the parents."

Imagine the youngsters' embarrassment. One of them, a 14-year-old boy, fired "My foot. Shits!" and walked off along with some of his friends.

The incidence highlights how teenagers and the adults drift apart over something which comes quite natural and which needs appreciation rather than criticism from the elders. Freud has called such adult reactions "downright cruel and unimaginative."

Why do adolescents resent parental disapproval of their "love"? They are puzzled why they are reprimanded for something which the mother and the father have in plenty ever since they can recall. They wonder what could be wrong in their "love". Is it some such thing that should neither be had nor talked about? Is "love" a shameful thing?

The parents must bear in mind that love between an adolescent boy and girl is not "just for kicks". Do not treat it too lightly. If still you do that, it is going to cost you quite a lot. It will cause a big communication "gap" between you and the teenager. Worst of all—remember, this gap is going to stay and trouble you all through the years to come. You surely would not relish it.

If you are a tactful parent, do not give him the chance to say, "I care two hoots for you. I know how to sort out the things on my own." For, the fact remains that, though he refuses to acknowledge it, he does need you. Make a wise and sensible reaction to his "love affairs".

And dissecting the "love affair" is the last thing you should do. Instead, encourage him to develop his relationship at home rather than keeping it a secret from you and demonstrating it to the world on the road or behind the bushes. Do not suspect that the young lovers will indulge in the "ultimate". They won't unless your attitude pushes them into precocious experiments.

Most adolescent "love affairs", don't you forget, are more of emotional and idealistic attachments. Let these not be spoilt by your over-reaction. Right?

Teenager's crushes

A sizeable proportion of boys and girls become "mad" over a "fantasy individual"—say an actor, a singer or someone equally unattainable. The adored object—the "idol"—is used by the teenager as a "model" which becomes the basis of his future dreams.

Why does the teenager choose to fall in love with a particular person? His personality? No. His talent? No. His handsomeness? Again, no. It is his "unavailability". This cardboard figure would never be able to say to him "no" or "yes". So, he runs no risk of disappointment.

Researchers say that *crushes* are far more stronger and intense in girls. Girls are known to particularise the object of their devotion with greater intensity.

A boy may fill his room walls with sexy pictures. He would not be dying to know each and every detail about his "model" as girls do.

It would be silly if the parents fuss about crushes. They need to remember that the "idol" is a substitute for the mother or the father whom the teenager is now leaving behind in his attempt to untie the apron strings. More often than not, he is bound to cross this "turmoil" as and when the time comes.

A psychiatrist friend confides that only in rare instances where crushes continue into adult life and a point of no return seems to have reached that psychiatric intervention may be required. "That", as he puts it, "happens once in a blue moon in my experience."

Adolescent and parents

An impressive feature of the teenage period is that the adolescent tends to grow away from his parents. This happens in spirit and in body. A stage arrives when he looks at his own home as "no more than a pigeonhole" where he eats and sleeps and remains obsessed with his own body and the telephone. He spends a great deal of his time before the mirror.

When, at the dinner table or elsewhere parents express some sort of disapproval of his activities he becomes "difficult". He may feel miserable, calling his parents "stupid" and "old-fashioned". He may produce a remarkable "scene" with funny threats.

Swinging in mood is nearly always there. Some teenagers become secretive, refusing to come out of the egg-shell.

Since, he is all set to "revolt" against the parents and the *Establishment*—in fact, all sorts of *authoritarianism*—his chosen affiliations will run contrary to what the parents expect or wish. He may join an anti-social "gang" or become a staunch believer in religion or an atheist. Interest in games or school work will also boost or fall—just against the wishes of the elders. All this is an expression of a teenager's "protest", "revolt" and what he rightly or wrongly thinks his "independent power of deciding things as these should be".

There is more to the story. Reports about the teenagers getting not just abusive but starkly violent to the parents and grandparents are on the increase. A conscientious social worker, Ritu Khanna, tells me of how a 16-year-old boy abuses, hits, kicks and pushes his mother around, smashing furniture and what not. "Just because the poor mother is not able to buy him a mobike for very many months now," she clarifies, adding, "the mother will get mad some day."

Another middle-aged mother, an ex-model, has a shocking tale of perversion to tell. Says she: "My son, who is just past 12, frequently climbs up the bathroom ventilator to watch me taking a bath. When I caught him red-handed on at least two occasions, he shouted bloody four letter words at me.... I am at a loss to know how to sort it out."

Even these teenagers are in need of parental help and guidance. Don't wait, the teenager would not come and beg for it. You have got to volunteer it tactfully—without embarrassing him. Try to find out why he behaves as he does. Listen to him patiently rather than losing temper and over-reacting to his odd and irritating behaviour. Has he been misdirected by someone? Are you imposing on him school or college subjects that he does not like? Are you looking too much into his private life? Are you saying "no" rather too often?

Try to be truly present in your children's lives—of course without being overprotective or fussy. And ensure an atmosphere of security and confidence.

For, make no mistake about it, there is no other way out to help him—which means to help yourself. Act today. Right away.

32

EXAMINATION FEVER

Several years ago, a middle-aged mother bumped into my outpatient room at the Postgraduate Institute of Medical Education & Research, Chandigarh, in a very agitated state.

"Look at this boy, Doc," she addressed me pointing at her 12-year-old son, "now that the exams are knocking at the door, the wretched headache never leaves him in peace. I don't really know what is going to happen."

After a thorough clinical work-up, all I could find was that the boy was extremely nervous with cold and clammy hands. All this plus his headache appeared to be related to his mother's threat a week back in such pernicious words as "and if you fail to top this time, you are doomed ... no pocket money, no top class dresses and no visits to the hill station... Understand?"

Performance anxiety

A consultation with the psychiatry colleagues confirmed my impression. The boy suffered from what we doctors call "performance anxiety". He was indeed scared he may not live up to his mother's expectations and then fall in his parents' grace.

I am quoting this situation not because it is so exclusive but because it represents classical mishandling of the child and his problems by the parents when the exams are round the corner. Recently, a team of doctors and psychologists of the *Child Health Study Group* conducted a countrywide survey about the behaviour and attitudes of school-going children during the period of 3 months prior to the final exams. At least 60 per cent of the participants were found to suffer from performance anxiety. Half of the sufferers were cited as having exaggerated manifestations as was the case with the child I have referred to a short while ago. The survey reports concludes that "mishandling by the parents, especially the overindulgent mothers, plays a key role in the sorry state of affairs".

The way out

Admittedly, exams are a fact of life. All children who are supposed to assure their future must come to terms that these have to be faced. The parents' anxiety whether the child is trying his utmost and whether he would make it to the top is quite understandable. But, in order that the child goes through a relaxed and healthier examination time, they must pay heed to the following "tips".

In the first place, ensure a peaceful, relaxed atmosphere so that he can concentrate well on his studies rather than indulge in confrontations with the parents or grandparents. Your concern for the child is understandable but, for Heaven's sake, don't show signs of anxiety. This is likely to be passed to the child, adding to his problems.

Secondly, provide ample encouragement to the child. "You're doing fine... if you make it like this, things may turn out still better" is a morale booster for the child and shows him the way to put his best foot forward. On the other hand, "O, you haven't finished this much even till now. How bad!" can be a grave negative force.

Respect the child's limits

Thirdly, do guide the child to prepare and put up his best but never pressurise him to attain beyond his reach. He has his limits which you must respect. Forcing him to go beyond that will be an invitation to troubles. In your fond pursuit to satisfy your overambitiousness, you may be causing irreparable damage to the child's mind.

Fourthly, as far as possible, discourage private tuitions. A certain mother had engaged four private tutors for her 10-year-old daughter, one each for English, Hindi, Maths and Science. The remaining couple of subjects were being taught to her by the mother herself. The little girl had a nervous breakdown days before the exams and had to see the year go down the drain rather than securing a top position in the class. That is it.

Fifthly, make sure you do not insist on continuous study hours. Give the child a couple of hours for relaxation and recreation. This will pay him dividends. After all, the brain and body both have their limits.

No bad comparisons please!

Sixthly, learn to motivate the child into studying in the appropriate manner. Rather than making such bad comparisons "if Ritu next door could stand first, why can't you, idiot?", "What a pity you are so poor whereas Meenu is shining," or "Sharmas are indeed lucky to have a son like Manu. Look at this rascal of ours", motivate the child by referring to such famous figures as Nehru, Einstein or Tolstoy. Your personalising the situation by bringing in the child next door is likely to cause fear in his mind. He may hate to gain through such an approach.

Seventhly, learn to give the child some gift etc. as a token of your appreciation for his hard work from time to time. As, for example, if he has finished his day's allotted work—never mind, even if it is little short of that—pass on the gift to him, saying "How very nice! You've worked hard enough. Hopefully you'll do better tomorrow."

Positive reinforcement pays

Last but not least, have the heart to reinforce the child positively. Even if she hasn't come up to your expectations, don't say, "What a pity you failed to come to our expectations". Why not say: "Well done, my daughter. I'm confident you will fare better next time."

Avoid street vendors

You must take special care of your child's diet during examination days. He needs extra proteins, energy and minerals. Try to make the food as pleasant and palatable as you can. Of course, you should avoid chillies. And, nothing from street vendors and hawkers if you are to safeguard the child from food poisoning. Right?

Anti-sleep pills too!

Bunty whose mother, Mrs. Praveen Joseph, met me at Roller Skating Rink sometime ago, would take an anti-sleep pill at about 9 p.m. during exam days and study as late as 2 or 3 a.m. "I do want him to do very well in his matric exams," she told me. "Can you believe the stimulant pill boosts his concentration and also prevents him from falling asleep." Today, Bunty's exams are over. Of course, he didn't do well enough. What is worse, his indulgence in drug menace has now gone too far.

Lesson? Never encourage your child to resort to drugs just to burn the midnight oil at exams time. Else, the drug abuse will eat the child inside out and upside down. Your own suffering won't be any less.

33
ADOPTION

1.   Mathurs are amongst the finest couples I have ever come across. Mr. Sudhir Mathur, 38, is an executive in a reputed firm whereas Mrs. Monika Mathur, 32, runs a painting school. Married for no less than 10 years, they are issueless, however. Both are very keen to bring up a child with love and devotion. "God has not been kind to us on this front," they confided to me one evening, "and, what is worse, the doctors are no longer hopeful we can have a child born to us."

2.   Patels, aged 40 and 32, have a school-going daughter of 10. Over the past many months they have grown terribly fond of a 5-year-old spastic boy in the nearby school for the handicapped. Often, the couple discuss if the little darling could be reared by them. Just as the daughter born to them is being brought up.

3.   At 40, Ms. Amita Sharma, a successful career woman, considers marriage out of question. Nevertheless, she is awfully eager to bring up a child with, as she says, "love, dedication and commitment". Just as if he is born to her.

4.   Mr. Surjit Singh Dhillon and his pretty wife, Poonam, were recently hit by a wretched tragedy. They lost botn children, aged 8 and 6, in a car accident. Very fond of children, they are in a fix as to what to do. "Life is losing meaning for us," Mrs. Poonam tells the visitors.

Adoption—yes, adoption—could well be the answer to the problems of all these folks.

What is adoption in precise terms? Well, adoption means bringing up a son or a daughter who was not born to you but who is legally now your issue and grows up under your loving care and security. The child, no doubt, satisfies your need and, perhaps, fills the vacuum in your life. At the same time, he needs to feel that he belongs to and is deeply and sincerely loved by you now and for all times to come-just as in the case of a biological child if you were to have one.

It is unfair to adopt a child with the aim of having a helper, to look after you when you grow old, or to hold back the hubby. Also, it is unwise to expect the adopted child to play a "ghost" for a child who has died. There is no point in adopting a child if one of the would-be parents is half-hearted and equivocal for adoption. The adopted child must belong completely and there must not be any element of ambivalence on the part of any of the parents.

What should be the age of the child to be adopted? The time-honoured rule is: the younger, the better. However, since older couples are now beginning to opt for adoption, the age of the adoptive child needs to match with that of the parents. A 10-year-old child may be fine for a couple in the late 30s or early 40s but he will undoubtedly be rather odd for a couple in their 20s.

A prospective adoptive parent may have apprehension about the social and genetic background of the child to be adopted. Remember that more than the social background of the original parents, it is the new environment and the sense of belonging that he is given which influence the personality development of the child. Such social ailments as delinquency, immorality or alcoholism are not inherited.

As regards the question of hereditary disorders, let it be borne in mind that these are, by any standard, infrequent. A small risk in adoption is certainly there. But, then, all human relationships carry some risk. Don't they?

The fixation for adopting a child of a relative is outright unfounded. More often than not, the child comes to know about his biological parents and is bound to be torn between two establishments. Not just that, the biological parents often claim him back at a later stage.

Likewise, it is not quite in order to take the child in adoption direct from the biological parents or through a third person who may choose to act funny sooner or later. The biological parents may someday try to get the child back, thereby ruining the happiness of the child as also of the adopting family.

All said and done, child adoption is best arranged through a noted child adoption agency. These agencies employ experienced workers to find the child most suited to the prospective adopting parents whose confidentiality is respected and who are not only helped in the process of completing legal formalities but also provided with emotional support during the waiting period.

Most adoption agencies, besides interviewing the prospective adopting parents on several occasions to find out how genuine their desire to adopt is and how much support they can offer to the child, ask for such documents as income certificate, health certificate and recommendation from three prominent citizens. Expenses to be incurred include service charges (depending on income), foster care charges and medical charges (incurred by the institution), court fee and lawyer's fees. The court stipulates one year follow-up action by the concerned agency. Once adoption becomes final, it is easy to obtain a new birth certificate with the child's new name and new parentage.

Never, make the mistake of keeping the adoption a secret from the child. He must know the truth as soon as he is old enough to understand. Parents must be clear on this point and speak to the child in some such way:

"It so happened that I grew increasingly keen to have a cute child with a fair complexion, black hair and brown eyes. So, I ran from pillar to post, looking for such a child. At long last, I went to an Agency and spoke to the person in-charge about my desire. The good lady brought me a child who was exactly what I had dreamed of. I said: 'O, goodness, what a darling' I shall adopt her, love her for ever as my child.' That was you."

This story will delight the child and give her a feeling of pride. This will project the positive side of adoption. In the years to come, she will come closer and closer to you, regarding her adoption by you as a mark of distinction.

To the query about the child's biological parents, you may answer thus:

"Well, somehow they were not in a position to take care of you. But, we were. And, now you are going to be ours for ever—yes, for all times to come."

Indian Association for Promotion of Adoption (IAPA)

The IAPA was launched in the year 1970 with the aim to:

1. Create a public platform for the need of a family for the child;

2. Create awareness of adoption, especially amongst Indians, both resident in India and abroad, so that abandoned/destitute children can find loving homes;

3. Promote uniform adoption legislation to enable minority communities as well as to adopt children legally.

Over the years, there has occurred a further expansion in the Association's objectives which may now be summarised as follows:

1. To endeavour to give children to a family who have none;
2. To awaken public opinion regarding the need and importance of a family for a child;
3. To create social climate for the promotion of adoption;
4. To promote appropriate legislation for adoption; safeguarding the rights of minors;
5. To assemble adoptive families for the purpose of sharing their experience and discussing their problems;
6. To promote and safeguard the interest of adoptive families and prospective adopters;
7. To collect information, literature and such other material as will increase knowledge concerning adoption;
8. To do such other things as are essential or conducive to the attainment of the aforesaid objectives of the Association.

The Association provides a place to which people could go for information and guidance. Its trained social workers can bring together the abandoned children and the prospective adoptive parents and counsel them on the procedures to be followed. The social workers also make a home study to make sure that only suitable children and parents are brought together.

If you wish to contact the Association, you may please note its address:

Indian Association for Promotion of Adoption,
Diners House, 1st Floor,
Veer Nariman Road,
Bombay-400023

Adoption: the legal position

What a pity that the existing adoption law is aimed for Hindus only and is miserably incomplete and no longer in line with the changing times! It often proves a bottleneck in the way of a prospective child to have a home, a family and dignity of being a respected citizen. As Mr. Mohinder Singh, a Supreme Court advocate puts it, "like the Special Marriage Act, there should be an enactment of a comprehensive Adoption Law applicable not only to one sect of persons but to all so that the children may be helped by the prospective parents."

I. Legal position for Hindus, including Sikhs, Jains, Buddhist

(a) Adoption of a child whose biological parents are alive. Section 10 of the Hindu Adoption and Maintenance Act, 1956, states that only a person, male or female, if he/she is Hindu and has not already been adopted, has not been married, and has not completed the age of 15 years (unless there is a custom or usage applicable to the parties to the adoption which permits persons who are married or have completed the age of 15 years) can be adopted by the person capable of adopting the Hindu child.

Who can adopt? According to the Act, any male Hindu who is of sound mind and is not a minor has the capacity to take a son or daughter in adoption, provided that, if he has a living wife, he shall not adopt without her consent, unless the wife has completely and finally renounced the world or ceased to be a Hindu or has been declared by a Court of competent jurisdiction to be of unsound mind.

Can a female adopt a child? Yes, provided that she is of sound mind and not a minor and not married, or, if married, whose marriage is dissolved or whose husband is dead or has completely and finally renounced the world or has ceased to be a Hindu, or has been declared by a Court of competent jurisdiction to be of unsound mind.

Who can give in adoption? According to the Act, only the father has the right to give the child in adoption. But, this right has to be exercised with the consent of the mother, unless the consent of the mother is unnecessary. If the father is not alive or he is not capable of exercising his right to give the child in adoption, the mother can give the child in adoption.

(B) Adoption of a child whose parents are dead, have completely and finally renounced the world, have abandoned the child, or have been declared by a court of competent jurisdiction to be of unsound mind or where the parentage of the child is not known. This category of children are usually left in hospitals, foundling homes or institutions of children. They need to be placed in suitable families which offer love, a sense of belonging and fine upbringing.

According to Section 9(4) of the Hindu Adoption and Maintenance Act, 1956, the existing guardian of such a child may give the child in adoption either to himself or to another person with the permission of the Court which must satisfy itself that the adoption would be in the best interest and welfare of the child. No person, either adopting or giving in adoption, can give/receive or promise to give/receive any payment or reward in consideration of adoption except such as the court may sanction.

II. Legal position for non-Hindus

Under the provision of Guardian and Wards Act, 1980, a person other than a Hindu can also be appointed as guardian of the child provided the Court is satisfied that the appointment of a guardian, of the minor is in the interest and welfare of the child. The Court also has the right to revoke the appointment of a guardian, if in its opinion, the appointment of the guardian is no longer in the interest and welfare of the child.

34

THE SICK CHILD: AN OVERVIEW

The parents must learn to identify that the child is sick early enough. Which means that they should be familiar with common symptoms of acute and chronic illnesses in childhood as given below. They should be able to recognise when the situation is serious enough and look up the doctor in the hospital or in his private clinic.

Recognition of acute illness

You should always take notice of the following manifestations of acute illness:

— Refusal to take feed
— Excessive weeping without any apparent cause
— Persistent vomiting
— Fever
— Persistent cough
— Drowsiness/unconsciousness
— Excessive irritability
— Neck or body stiffness
— Fits
— Diarrhoea/dysentery
— Persistent pain in any part of the body
— Skin rash
— Sore throat
— Hoarseness
— Running nose
— Difficult breathing
— Jaundice
— Swelling over feet or round the eyes
— Sudden development of pallor
— Blood in urine

As you wait for the doctor...

You are indeed lucky if the doctor is immediately available. But, very frequently, it may be quite sometime before the doctor's advice becomes available.

In that event, do keep your cool. Getting panicky will only multiply your and your child's problems and solve nothing. A particular mother got so scared on seeing her 2-year-old daughter having convulsions that she herself fainted, adding to the poor husband's problems. In another case, the parents, rather than looking after their 1-year-old baby with high fever, ended up quarrelling between themselves, blaming and counter-blaming each other for the child's illness.

In the first place, it is quite natural to let the child lie down in a cosy place if you find that he is not well. You need not force him to bed. All that is needed is "rest". He may like to sit in a chair.

Secondly, give him playthings and reading material to while away his time and keep boredom at a distance.

Thirdly, relax discipline. Give him extra affection and make it a point to be personally in attendance to his needs. This will give him reassurance and security. Tell him that his problem is a passing phase and that he will be well and kicking about soon. While you keep him cheerful and look after his emotional needs, prepare him for the doctor's consultation which he should happily look forward to.

If the child has a high fever, it is better to give him a tepid sponge— not just over the forehead but all over the body. You may give him aspirin or paracetamol in a dose suggested by the doctor on an earlier occasion or on telephone.

If the child has vomiting and diarrhoea, do not make the common mistake of starving him. Instead, give him plenty of sips of oral fluid.

In fact, in any sick child, you should take care of the child's nutrition. Lots of oral fluids and soft food, such as milk, soup, bread, khichri, curd, banana, fruit juice, are time-honoured favourites. Of course, never push food. That only irritates the child and causes antagonism, leading to difficulties in management of his illness.

As you wait for the doctor, take notice of various symptoms that you have encountered. You will be asked by him about them. If the child has been vomiting and has diarrhoea, always save a sample of the vomitus and stools for his inspection and examination. It is in order to save a sample of urine as well. In many cases, urine examination is routinely done by the doctors.

35

CERTAIN MEDICAL PROBLEMS

If you are under the impression that this section is aimed at teaching you how to do little of "doctoring", you are sadly mistaken. All I want is to provide some guidelines to enable you to understand some of the child's medical problems. I expect you to report to your doctor, preferably a child specialist (pediatrician), for exact diagnosis and management of the ailment.

Eye ailments

Blocked tear duct (nasolacrimal duct blockade) may manifest in the form of persistent watery discharge (since normal secretions from the eye fail to reach the nose) and even inflammation of the eye, the so-called "conjunctivitis". It is usually due to simple congenital obstruction of the duct and clears spontaneously by 1 to 3 months of age. All that is needed is frequent washing of the eye with a moist sterile swab and gentle massage of the skin overlying the tear duct. In the presence of an infection, your doctor may prescribe antimicrobial eye drops. In case the blockade persists in later months, the ophthalmologist (eye doctor) may decide to open the duct by a small surgical operation. This operation is usually undertaken after the child has reached the age of 2 years.

Black eye means swelling and bruising of the tissues surrounding the eye. This needs no special treatment, except for hot fomentation, and it disappears in a few days time.

Foreign body, as long as it is small, is likely to be washed out by the tears. If that has not happened, try to wash it out with cold water. You must not try to manually remove it on your own.

Chemical burns need to be treated by washing out the eyes with plenty of cold water before medical help becomes available.

Stye is a tiny eruption in the hair follicle of an eyelash. The area becomes red, tender and swollen. Application of local heat helps in breaking and draining it. If styes occur in crops with recurrences, you must see the ophthalmologist. He may like to rule out visual errors and diabetes mellitus.

Eye allergy, say to pollen, grass, house dust etc, may cause redness, itchiness and watering of the white conjunctiva as also swelling of the lids and the pouches beneath the eyes. Accompanying allergic manifestations may include cough, wheezing and running, itching nose. Besides giving an appropriate treatment, the doctor may like to have certain tests conducted to find out the offending allergen.

Conjunctivitis (red eye), meaning inflammation of the membranes lining the eye, is characterised by redness, itching, pain, discharge and stickiness of eyelids, particularly on waking up in the morning. It responds well to antibiotic drops or ointment put two to three times in each eye.

Trachoma, a sort of chronic conjunctivitis, is a viral disease. It is a very common problem in our country, particularly because of the widespread bad practice of putting kajal with the same slim metallic instrument in several children and adults. With the eradication of smallpox, it is now the top cause of preventable blindness in this country.

Cross eye (squint) is normal during the first few weeks of life. But if your baby continues squinting after he is 3 months old, you must consult a good eye specialist for confirmation of diagnosis and correct management. The treatment is usually in the form of eye exercises, correction of vision by wearing glasses and surgical operation. Remember that delay in correction of squint beyond the age of 4 or 5 years may cost the child his one eye.

Eye fatigue or *strain* is generally reflected in the form of headache in the afternoon or evening, difficulty in reading what is written on the blackboard, difficulties with school work, redness of the eyes, blinking, dislike of light etc. The usual cause is myopia. Do not hesitate in carrying out the doctor's instructions even if the child has to wear glasses at a very young age.

Night blindness is the earliest manifestation of vitamin A deficiency. It is easy to treat it at this stage. Else, the condition may worsen eventually causing blindness.

Ear ailments

Wax formed in the ear usually tempts mothers (more so grandmothers) to put warm oil in the ear and to clean the ear canal with a matchstick, hairpin, allpin or a pencil. This is a dangerous practice and must stop. I have seen several children whose ear canals are damaged in this way. If you indeed feel that wax is troubling the child quite a lot, you should look up the ENT specialist who knows how to solve your problem best.

Do not ever manipulate the foreign body accidentally pushed into the child's ear on your own. See the doctor.

Acute dishcarge from one or both ears is usually secondary to an upper respiratory catarrh. It may cause considerable pain. Of course, prompt medical treatment is needed. If left untreated, it may progress to what we doctors call as *subacute otitis media.*

Severe ear pain (so much that the child may not allow you to touch his ear) may be secondary to a boil or inflammation in the ear canal, the so-called *otitis externa.*

Remember that neglect in attending to the child's ear problems may result in deafness.

Also, do not forget to get your child's ear examined for partial or total deafness, if he has not learnt to talk by the time he has reached the normal age for speech.

Nose and throat ailments

Any child having perpetual cough and running nose needs to be examined for *chronic sinusitis* by a specialist.

Such a child should also be examined for large swollen glands at the back of the nose. The so-called *adenoids* are known to cause mouth breathing. The child keeps the mouth open, more so during sleep. His face takes up typical configuration. He becomes dull in studies. Removal of the adenoids surgically is the right answer. The operation is simple and the sooner the child gets over it, the better.

Many children get into the bad habit of frequently pricking the nose. This often causes nose bleed (*epistaxis*) by injuring the most profusely blood supplied area called *Little's point*. Besides nose picking, causes of nose bleed include excessive dryness of nasal mucosa as in hot, dry weather, infection, injury, blowing the nose very hard and bleeding disorders. In some cases, there may be no particular reason for nose bleed at all.

In case of nose bleed, make the child sit with his face and head tilted forward. Then pinch his nose with your thumb and index finger for a few minutes. Or place some ice against the back of head and neck, forehead, or on the nose. These manoeuvres stop the bleeding following the formation of a clot over the bleeding point. Later, you may consult a doctor. If the bleeding continues despite your first aid, the child needs to be rushed to the hospital. He may have to be cauterised. The process consists in burning the exposed blood vessel.

Inflammation of tonsils, the two pieces of lymphatic tissue lying at the back of the throat is known as *tonsillitis*. Just the big size of the tonsils has no meaning and need not frighten you. Manifestations of tonsillitis include sore throat, fever and malaise. The glands appear red and angry. Its usual cause is a bacterial (streptococcal) infection. Therapy with penicillin or an alternative drug proves very effective.

Some children get frequent attacks of tonsillitis. I, like most pediatricians, do not subscribe to the view that early removal of tonsils decidedly stops further throat infections or that it accelerates the child's growth or it cures allergic attacks. If, however, they are the cause of constant attacks of tonsillitis—at least three each winter—and ill-health of the child, it may be advisable to get them removed.

Common cold is by far the commonest viral infection. It is characterised by nasal discharge or stuffiness, slight fever, sneezing and uneasiness. Breathing difficulty may cause feeding problem, irritability and sleeplessness. Pain in the ear is frequent. Headache and bodily pains may be there in grown-up children.

Superimposed bacterial infection is quite likely to occur in a child with common cold. The infection, if not timely controlled, may trickle down into the lungs.

As your doctor will tell you, as yet there is no real treatment for cold. He may prescribe aspirin or paracetamol, an antihistaminic and some nasal drops for symptomatic relief. On your part, try to keep the child's nose clean and expose him to steam inhalation two to three times a day.

And, yet, remember that it has been well said that: *If you treat cold it takes seven days to cure; if you leave it as such, it lasts just a week.*

Croup, a viral infection of the voice box, manifests as hoarseness, breathlessness and dry, tight, barking cough. You should place the child in moist air. This can be achieved at home by sitting in the bathroom with hot shower running and the doors closed. Meanwhile, arrangements to seek medical advice should be made.

Hay fever is an allergic reaction of the lining of the nose and sinuses around it to some allergen, say pollen, house-dust, house-mite or danger from a pet. Manifestations include nasal congestion, sneezing, clear nasal discharge and itching of the nose and eyes. The attacks may be seasonal. Treatment is primarily symptomatic with reduction in child's exposure to the offending allergen.

Chest infection

Bronchitis is inflammation of the windpipe and its branches and sub-branches in the lungs. Its manifestations include cough (which may be severe enough, interfering with feeding and sleep), cold and fever.

Pneumonia is inflammation of the air cells (alveoli) of the lung. Besides, cold, cough and fever, the child usually has some breathing difficulty which is likely to worsen unless prompt intervention is made. The child is usually quite sick. He may have chest pain as well.

It is possible that your doctor advises you to get the child hospitalised for pneumonia. Perhaps, the child's breathing difficulty has warranted administration of oxygen. Mild bronchitis and pneumonia are generally treated at home, provided that the child is not very young and malnourished in which case these diseases can be very dangerous.

Mind you, there is no truth in the commonly-held belief that banana, orange, curd or milk cause pneumonia.

Bronchiolitis is a serious disease of infants in which there is inflammation of the bronchioles (the minute air passages in the lungs), usually as a result of a viral infection. Following a mild upper respiratory infection, the infant develops breathlessness, fever and cyanosis with or just a mild or no cough. If delay in instituting proper treatment occurs, dehydration and electrolyte imbalance may supervene. Even heart failure may occur. Don't delay transportation of such a child to the hospital where doctors are in a position to treat it well by giving oxygen and intravenous fluids in addition to other measures.

Asthma

It is the result of allergy of the respiratory tract to certain agent(s). There is production of contraction of the air passages in the lungs (*bronchospasm*) so that the child can breathe in (inhale) easily but breathing out (exhalation) becomes difficult.

Asthma usually starts at 2 to 6 years of age. In a typical attack, which begins in the early hours of the morning, the child sits up in bed and begins to cough, producing lots of wheezing. An upper respiratory infection may precede the attack.

Asthmatic attacks get less severe as the child grows. Many a time, cases are spontaneously cured as puberty sets in or when the climate and environment is changed.

An asthmatic child should always be under regular treatment of a doctor. The doctor will prescribe medicines. But, on your part, you should also see that his emotional needs are met and that he is encouraged to live a normal life. House dust is the greatest enemy of an asthmatic child. Try to keep his room dustfree. Also avoid the child's playing with pet animals. Breathing exercises, like blowing a balloon, help to prevent damage to the respiratory tract.

Lastly, cooperate with the doctor if he wishes to refer the child to a more sophisticated centre like Patel Chest Institute, New Delhi, to carry out a series of skin tests to find out the "allergen" and, if needed, to desensitise the child against it.

Heart disease

If your baby has not been thriving well, develops frequent chest infection, has breathing difficulty on little exertion or develops attacks of blue lips and fingers and toenails and has club-shaped fingers and toes, report to the doctor. He may be suffering from a *congenital heart disease*. There are two major types: 1. *Cyanotic*, in which cyanosis (blue colour) is the major manifestation. 2. *Acyanotic*, in which there is persistence of an opening between the left and the right sides of the heart but no cyanosis occurs unless the disease is fairly advanced.

Your doctor would like to fully examine the child and then carry out investigations such as an electro-cardiogram (ECG), an X-ray chest and, if needed, cardiac catheterisation (it is done in only highly specialised centres) to confirm the diagnosis. For corrective surgery, you may have to be referred to a sophisticated institute.

The bigger serious threat to the young child's heart, however, comes from what is called *rheumatic fever*. Here, the child gets sore throat which is followed by pain and swelling in joints, fever and palpitations. The heart involvement may be immediate or the heart may take some time to be significantly affected. Immediate heart involvement usually causes heart failure. Permanent damage may be in the form of involvement of certain valves (mostly "mitral")—folds of membrane between right and left sides of the heart that permit flow of the blood in one direction only.

The proper diagnosis of rheumatic heart disease is made by clinical examination, laboratory tests, X-ray chest and ECG.

Your doctor would like to hospitalise such a child for adequate rest and management. On discharge, he will advise you to continue to give the child an injection of a long-acting penicillin (say Penidure LA-12) every 3 to 4 weeks to guard against relapses. Do not show any slackness in getting the child's regular check-up.

At times, a routine examination of your child may show a murmur in the heart. A murmur is an unusual sound (mind you, I didn't say "abnormal") heard on auscultation of the heart or great vessels. Don't fuss. It may well be nothing more than a functional murmur, having nothing to do with an organic heart problem. In 80 to 90 per cent instances it will disappear with passage of time. In any case, expert consultation to evaluate its nature will be in order.

Thrush

If you see a white, thick coating on the tongue and over the lips and cheeks, chances are that your baby has fungus infection of the oral cavity. It is usually seen in undernourished children, particularly with poor hygiene, and is quite painful, causing interference in feeding. Children on antibiotics are prone to it.

Application of 0.5 per cent gentian violet liberally 2 to 3 times a day cures it in 2 to 3 days' period.

Diarrhoea

If your child's bowel habit has suddenly changed and he has begun to pass loose stools with increased frequency, with or without mucus or blood, he is, in all probability, suffering from acute diarrhoea.

Diarrhoea seldom occurs in breast-fed babies. It is, however, common in babies fed on unhygienic, diluted, dirty formula fed with a bottle. The cause is usually an infection which may be bacterial or viral.

What damages most in diarrhoea is the continuous loss of considerable fluids and salts from the body. Since vomiting is often associated, fluid and salt loss gets further aggravated. The effects of diarrhoea and vomiting, the so-called *gastroenteritis*, are worst in malnourished children and in early infancy.

The loss of fluid and salt from the body is called *dehydration*. Its earliest manifestation is thirst and irritability. The abdomen becomes distended and the mucous membrane of the mouth turns dry. The skin becomes dry and inelastic. Eyes are sunken. If anterior fontanelle (a diamond shaped gap in the front portion of the head) is still open, it becomes depressed. If allowed to progress, the child may stop passing urine, have respiratory difficulty and go into shock and unconsciousness. This stage of severe dehydration may kill the child.

You should be vigilant and look up the doctor before significant dehydration has set in. Meanwhile, give the child plenty of oral fluids. If vomiting is complicating the picture, do not push fluids. Just give sips at frequent intervals. You may buy a packet of rehydration mixture. Or prepare it by mixing half a teaspoonful of common salt, 5 teaspoonfuls of sugar and a little of orange or lemon juice in a litre of boiled and cooled water. Generally speaking, you should give two glasses of this solution to a child below 6 months, three glasses to a child between 6 months and one year and four glasses beyond this age. Continue breast-feeding or whatever artificial feeding you had been giving unless it seems to be worsening the baby's diarrhoea. Adding curd and banana to the intake will be of added advantage.

Signals for medical attention in diarrhoea

1. Failure to pass urine for over 6 hours
2. Persistent vomiting so that the child is unable to retain anything
3. Abdominal distension
4. High fever
5. Diarrhoea lasting over 2 days
6. Passage of blood or mucus in motions
7. Obvious signs of dehydration
8. Drowsiness, unconsciousness or shock

As soon as possible, consult the doctor. If the diarrhoea is not severe and dehydration is mild, he would like you to get the child treated at home. Of course, he may prescribe some medicine for symptomatic control of diarrhoea and a chemotherapeutic agent if he feels that diarrhoea is of bacterial origin.

In case of moderate to severe dehydration, he is likely to admit the child to the hospital for intravenous administration of fluids. Hospitalisation may also be indicated if vomiting is persistent and oral rehydration is difficult.

Vomiting

We have just talked how vomiting associated with gastroenteritis may cause dehydration and the pressing need to control it.

Vomiting is seldom a problem in a breast-fed baby but may occur if the baby on the bottle drinks milk fast or if the teat hole is far too large. Failure to do regular burping is another common cause.

Vomiting may be associated with whooping cough (*kali khansi*), forced feeding, indigestion, food or other poisoning or tonsillitis.

A forceful *projectile vomiting* in a baby around 4 weeks of age is usually due to congenital narrowing of the outlet of the stomach (*pyloric stenosis*). It needs surgical treatment.

Intestinal parasites

Does your child suffer from recurrent pain in the tummy? Is he going downhill? Or has his weight been constant whereas he should have been gaining it over the months or a year or so? Has there been an increase or decrease in his appetite? Does he suffer from frequent bowel upset—usually diarrhoea but at times constipation? Does he eat dirt or paint flakes? Does he suffer from irritability, perianal itching or sleeplessness? Is he becoming pale?

If the answer to some or all of these queries is "yes", your child perhaps suffers from presence of worm(s) in the digestive system. There are many varieties of such worms. The common ones are roundworm, threadworm, giardia, amoeba, kookworm and dwarf tapeworm. whipworm, strongyloides, and tenia solium and saginata are relatively uncommon.

Except for threadworm and roundworm which you may recognise in the child's stools, your doctor would like to have testing of child's stools on at least three successive days for diagnosis of the particular worm infestation the child is suffering from. In many instances, children suffer from more than one infestation, the so-called *polyparasitism*.

Follow the doctor's instructions as far as treatment is concerned. But, remember that in our country worm infestation is more or less a family disease. It will be necessary to treat other affected members of the family about the same time.

Also, make a note that intestinal parasitic disease is always secondary to poor hygienic conditions and contaminated water and footstuffs. Ensure attention to these factors. Further, see that everybody in the family wears shoes habitually and uses sanitary toilet.

Anaemia

Deficiency of the red coloring pigment in the blood (haemoglobin), usually due to iron deficiency, causes what the doctors refer to as anaemia.

The anaemic child looks pale, lethargic and listless. Pallor is more readily identified by looking at the conjunctiva lining the eyelids, finger nils and mucous membrane of the mouth. In significant anaemia, the child becomes breathless on exertion.

The commonest cause of anaemia in Indian children is poor. diet. Intestinal parasites, particularly the great blood sucker, *Hookworm*, is the close runner-up. Sudden loss of blood as in an accidental bleeding, destruction of red cells, less blood formation by the bone marrow or chronic infections are other factors that cause anaemia.

It is uncommon for infants under 6 months to develop significant anaemia. Thanks to the iron stores that the baby gets from the mother! After this age the baby must have supplements of iron. Else, he is likely to develop anaemia. Don't forget that milk, no matter whether it is mother's or cow's, is a poor source of iron. Early introduction of semi-solids, say after 3 months, helps to provide sufficient iron to meet the child's needs later when the maternal stores have exhausted. Starting the infant on iron drops at 3 to 4 months makes the things fool-proof.

Your doctor would do a blood test to find the extent and type of anaemia that your child is suffering from. In some cases he may like to do bone marrow and some other tests.

Generally, the doctor would prescribe iron tablets, drops or syrup to treat your child's anaemia. If it is severe, he may like to give iron by injection(s).

The parents will do well to cooperate with the doctor in finding out and properly treating the operative factor(s) for anaemia. It is useless to push iron and leave hookworm (to continue to suck child's blood) untreated.

Also, do encourage the child to eat iron-containing foods such as green leafy vegetables, egg yolk, molasses, red meat (liver, kidney and heart) and wholegrain cereals.

Malaria

What a pity that malaria which had been practically eradicated for over 15 years returned with a big bang in India in the 1970s. More recently, the disease has begun to show decline, however.

Malaria results from the bite of an infected female mosquito of the species *Anopheles*. March to October seems to be the mosquito season in India.

Malaria is characterised by high fever (with or without rigors and shivering) which is sudden in onset. It remains there for some hours. When the temperature begins to come down, the child sweats enormously. Often fever is also accompanied by body pains, especially headache, loss of appetite and general feeling of being not well. At times, malaria fever may present just like influenza.

Occasionally, malaria caused by a special kind of parasite, *Plasmodium falciparum*, may invade the brain, causing fits and unconsciousness. The is called *cerebral malaria*.

According to current practice, doctors, as soon as they suspect this disease, take a blood sample, prepare a film on a slide from it and look for presence of the parasite under a microscope. Chloroquine is given to each one of the suspected cases. But, if the blood film confirms presence of malarial parasite, the patient is also given a 5-day course of another drug, primaquine.

Fo cerebral malaria, it is desirable to get the child admitted to the hospital. In such cases, chloroquine is given not by mouth but by an injection into the muscle mass or a vein.

You must protect your child against mosquito bites during the summer and rainy seasons. Ask the municipal authorities to clean the possible breeding places (say pools of stagnant water) for mosquitoes in your neighbourhood. Keep your house tidy and get DDT sprayed in it. It is advisable to use mosquito nets during nights.

Moreover, it will be a good practice to give each and every member of the family (including children below 1 year) a prophylactic dose of chloroquine once a week during March-October.

Tuberculosis

"Does TB occur in small children at all, doctor?" is an oft-asked question by the parents who are under the impression that tuberculosis is a disease of the old. Yes, tuberculosis does affect children though its presentation in this age group is quite different.

Tuberculosis is caused by a bacterial organism, *Mycobacterium tuberculosis*. In order that the tuberculous infection affects the child, he has got to be exposed to prolonged contact with someone, in the house or in the neighbourhood, suffering from the disease. That someone may not necessarily be a parent, a brother or a sister or a relative. It may well be a servant, a cook or an ayah. Such an infecting person usually discharges tuberculous bacilli in the sputum.

Childhood tuberculosis may affect any part of the body. Generally, however, it chooses the lungs and the lymph glands—anywhere, including neck, armpit, groin and abdomen. Its most serious form involves the brain, causing *tuberculous meningitis*.

Remember that the doctor is fully justified to suspect tuberculosis in your child and to investigate it if the child has prolonged fever without any apparent cause, if the child suffers from recurrent cough and/or respiratory disease, if he is malnourished or suffers from failure to thrive or if he develops enlargement of the glands (in the neck and elsewhere) that fails to subside in due course on its own or with treatment. A known history of contact with a tuberculous patient too justifies such investigation; so does the persistent and significant glandular enlargement in the armpit following BCG vaccination. Insidious onset of vomiting, neck stiffness, fits, loss of consciousness-suggesting tuberculous meningitis—also warrants such investigations.

Investigations for diagnosis of tuberculosis include a skin test (tuberculin or Mantoux test; *BCG diagnostic test*) and X-ray chest. If tuberculosis of brain is on the card, the doctor will obtain fluid from lower part of the spine for testing in addition to other investigations. Do not panic over it. It is a safe procedure. In case of glandular swellings, a bit of gland is often surgically cut (*glandular biopsy*), processed and then examined microscopically for evidence of tuberculosis.

Finally, do not get shocked when the doctor makes the diagnosis of tuberculosis in your child. Take it easy and cooperate with him in carrying out anti-tuberculous treatment religiously for several months, the exact duration varying with the treatment regimen.

Enteric (typhoid) fever

Oh yes, typhoid fever certainly occurs in young children in our part of the world.

The disease is caused by a bacterial organism, *Salmonella typhi*. It results from contaminated food, unboiled milk, vegetables or water. Housefly plays a significant role by carrying the infection from urine or stools of an active sufferer or carrier of the disease to the foodstuff, thus making it eminently conducive for others to get infected. Do not encourage children to go out for ice-cream, *kulfi, chat* etc., sold without any respect to hygiene at the roadside stalls. The same holds good for commercially-sold ice.

The peak incidence of typhoid occurs in summer and rainy season when fly population shows enormous rise.

The child has a moderate to high fever, usually around 102°F. This fever continues despite symptomatic treatment with antipyretic agents. The appetite is lost or considerably reduced, the tongue gets coated, some drowsiness is usual (in fact, the very meaning of the term "typhoid" is cloudiness of consciousness.) and the child looks sick and toxic. Headache, vomiting, abdominal pain and distension and anaemia are frequently present. Unlike an adult, typhoid in a child usually causes little diarrhoea rather than constipation.

While the doctor prescribes treatment, which you should give to the child as directed, do not get nervous if the fever does not subside immediately. As a normal response, it is expected to take a few days. Also take care of the child's nutrition. There is no truth in the saying that such a child should not be given semi-solids and solids. In fact, he should be given. Of course, he would prefer to take soft foods such as khichri, khir, custard, banana, mangoes, mosumbis, curd, milk, and egg to start with. Give him plenty of juice and soup but do not stick to just the liquids. What he needs is normal nutritious diet—that includes chapati and meat—and the earlier you give that to the child, the better.

No, you do not have to insist on the child's sticking to the bed once fever is over. Rest is important during convalescence as well but it need not be strict bed-rest.

Viral hepatitis

Imagine, one day your child is found to have lemon-like yellow eyes. He refuses to eat and complains of tummy pain and vomiting. He has slight fever too.

Well, wait, he is suffering from what the medical profession technically calls "viral hepatitis". The disease is caused by a virus present in contaminated food or water. It often takes epidemic proportion in various parts of India and other developing countries.

As soon as you suspect the disease in your child, report to your doctor. He will get his urine examined and confirm the diagnosis.

During acute stage you must give the child as much rest as possible. The doctor will direct you to give one of the liver tonics to the child regularly, to give him carbohydrate-rich diet, plenty of glucose (sugarcane juice is excellent), fruit juices etc. Excessive use of protein and fat is not encouraged. With this dietetic regimen, the child's appetite soon improves and the begins to take normal diet.

Recovery from viral hepatitis is usually complete.

Diphtheria

If your child has developed sore throat, hoarseness of voice and a greyish white membrane in the throat, over the tonsils in particular, look up the doctor. This may well be diphtheria, a highly contagious disease that, if not immediately tackled, may kill.

The doctors confirm diagnosis of diphtheria by taking a swab from the throat and examining it microscopically for the said organisms. If confirmed, the child is immediately administered a calculated dose of antidiphtheria serum by injection and also use regular 3 to 4 daily doses of an antibiotic such as penicillin or erythromycin.

The greatest danger of diphtheria lies in the white membrane extending lower down into the windpipe and causing obstruction to normal breathing. The resultant respiratory distress may warrant an emergency operation called *tracheostomy*, to ensure continuity of breathing.

Pertussis (whooping cough)

It begins as an ordinary cough for about a week. Then, in the second week, bouts of cough become more and more prolonged. The child's face becomes red (flushed) and he vomits. As the bout is at its fag end, the child takes a deep breath, producing a croaky noise. This is the "whoop".

Remember, that even a newborn can suffer from whooping cough, which results from an infection by the bacterium, *B. pertussis*. He may not, however, demonstrate that typical "whoop".

Also, remember that triple vaccine does not absolutely protect against the whooping cough. Of course, a vaccinated child, if affected, will get only a mild attack of the disease.

Besides administering the medicines prescribed by the doctor, see that you feed him well. Vomiting is a real problem. So, give the child small feeds in between the bouts and more frequently. Else, he will get malnourished since, despite prompt treatment, the disease takes several weeks to get under control.

Tetanus (lock jaw)

Children frequently keep falling by the roadside, injuring themselves, or suffering from rusted nail punctures in the bodies. If they have not been properly vaccinated with triple vaccine early in life, such accidents pose a serious threat to their lives in the form of what is known as *tetanus*.

Tetanus may also occur in a newborn if his umbilical cord has not been cut with clean, sterilised scissors or knife or if he is born at a contaminated place.

The child with tetanus develops stiffness of the jaw muscles so that he finds it very difficult to open it (*lock jaw*). He cannot chew and swallow food.

The stiffness of the back muscles may lead to the arching of the body (*opisthotonos*). A minor stimulus may cause spasms or fits during which the child becomes miserable.

Unfortunately, once tetanus has developed, doctors find themselves in a very helpless state. They cannot do a thing to save the child in a large majority of the cases. That is why, you, as a good mother, must make sure that your child has received full vaccination. In case of a roadside injury, never skip asking the doctor if tetanus toxoid is to be given or not.

Further, if you are expecting another baby, ensure that the doctor gives you an injection of tetanus toxoid during pregnancy.

Poliomyelitis

This is a viral disease that affects by entry of the contaminated water or food into the digestive tract. A great deal of physical handicaps in our country appear to be secondary to an attack of poliomyelitis in childhood.

The disease starts with fever and pains in the limbs. At times there may be stiffness of the neck and back. After a few days, it is noted that the child has developed weakness of one leg or any part of the body. Occasionally, the disease may advance to involve the muscles controlling breathing and kill the child.

When you suspect occurrence of poliomyelitis, put him to bed before you can have the doctor about to confirm the impression. If it is indeed what you thought, the doctor will ask you to continue the bed-rest as long as there is local pain and tenderness. He will also prescribe a pain-killing drug. He will advise you against administration of any injection to the child by another physician or a quack. Mind you, giving injection can aggravate the muscle damage.

Once the child is out of the acute phase, he should have exercises and physiotherapy to obtain as much positive function as possible. Remember, that physiotherapy would have to be continued over a long time. You must show patience and keep your cool so that the child feels encouraged during this period. Your over-anxiety and cursing the fate will not be the answer to his problem.

Measles

This viral disease usually starts with a running nose, watering of the eyes, cough and fever. This phase, in which the child looks quite indisposed, lasts for 3 to 4 days. A remarkable observation during this phase is the flushing of the face. This phase soon gives way to appearance of a fine reddish rash, resembling lots of insect bites, over the face. Soon the rash spreads to other parts of the body. In a couple of days, rash as well as fever begin to subside.

As your doctor would tell you, all that you need to give the baby with simple measles is paracetamol; cold sponging and frequent washing of the eyes in case of excessive watering do the child a lot of good. Do not neglect his fluid and nutritional needs.

What you must not forget is that very often the child with measles may suffer from such complications as chest, ear and throat infection. Very rarely, the measles virus may invade the brain, causing encephalitis which is likely to result in mental retardation and disability.

In case of complications, the doctor will advise you to give specific treatment. You must carry out his instructions. It will be stupid not to give the medicines in the belief that these may suppress the rash or that the act may offend the Goddess whose effect the disease is regarded by many conservative people.

Ask your doctor as to what to do about other children in the family. He may give them injections of gamma globulins so that, in case they also get measles, the attack is mild and there are no serious complications.

Chickenpox

With the total eradication of smallpox from the world, we are left with at least one disease that, though less dangerous, resembles it in more than one way. That is chickenpox.

This viral disease starts with fever, lassitude and headache followed by appearance in a couple of days of a rash on the trunk. It becomes a blister soon. The blister gradually takes the shape of a scab. Appearance of new crops of blisters and their scabbing continues for 2 to 3 days. Thus at a time you may see different types of rashes. Associated with the rash is a lot of itching.

No, chickenpox needs no treatment. Application of calamine lotion to the rash and antihistaminic medicine to relieve itching usually suffice.

Remember, chickenpox rash is predominantly over the trunk, there is no vaccination to prevent it and it leaves no permanent marks on the body.

Mumps

This again is a viral disease and is, as a rule, not a serious problem.

The main symptoms are painful swelling of the parotid glands which are situated in front of the ears. On chewing and swallowing, the child complains of pain. Mild fever is usually present. At times the parotid gland involvement may be only one-sided.

Mumps does not need much of a treatment. Paracetamol may be given to relieve pain and fever. Spicy foods should be avoided for a few days or excessive secretion of saliva may aggravate local pain and tenderness.

Remember to report to the doctor if the child with mumps complains of pain in the tummy or painful swelling of testes. The former suggests involvement of the pancreas and the latter inflammation of the testes-the two well-known but infrequent complications of the disease.

Skin ailments

Nappie rash is a red and slightly rough rash over the nappie area of the infant whose nappies are not changed often enough. It is a kind of dermatitis caused by ammonia which is known to be very irritating to the infant's skin. The rash is susceptible to a superadded bacterial or fungal infection which may further complicate the picture. Once the rash has appeared, treatment consists in exposing the affected area to warm, dry area during daytime. At night, a zinc oxide ointment may be applied. In case of a superadded infection, the doctor would like to give a specific treatment. The most important preventive measure, as you can appreciate, is nappie care. Change wet or dirty nappie as soon as you notice it. Leave nappie off at times so that air finds an access to the skin.

Urticaria (nettle rash), an allergic condition, manifests as very irritating "wheals" that may blend to involve large areas of body. Rash is frequently noticed after a warm bath, around pressure points of the body. A localised form of urticaria is called "angioneurotic oedema". It may involve lips or some other parts of face, penis or larynx. The swelling is over, as a rule, in a matter of hours. Local application of calamine lotion and anti-allergic pill/injection gives gratifying results. In our country, roundworm infection of the gut is a leading cause of urticaria and the doctors usually like to exclude this possibility.

Insect bite is usually a minor problem, causing only local itching. Nevertheless, in allergic children, severe reactions in the form of asthma, shock or hives may result. Cold compresses, calamine lotion and anti-allergic therapy controls the itching and swelling in minor cases. Children with breathlessness or shock may need hospitalisation.

Prickly heat refers to a fine pinkish rash which itches. The rash is usually more marked over the neck but may be present anywhere on the body. It is a common problem with babies during the summer months.

The best precaution is to put minimum clothes on the baby, give him frequent bath with cold water and keep him in cool environment. Application of calamine lotion or a good quality prickly heat powder, such as *Mycoderm*, all over the body, not only prevents it, but also cures it.

Scabies is an infection by a little parasite. It is highly contagious and generally found in almost all the family members. The characteristic lesion consists of pinhead-sized pimple which is mostly found between fingers to begin with but later spreads all over the body. The constant itching is very troublesome.

If you really want to get rid of it, treat all family members at the same time. As your doctor would tell you, the affected person should apply the prescribed medicine (say *Ascabiol* or *Crotorax*) liberally all over the body after taking a bath. Next day, another application is given but without a bath and the individual made to wear the same clothes. Next day, i.e., the third day, he takes a good bath and wears fresh, washed and ironed clothes.

All the clothes, including bedsheet and pillow covers, must be boiled and washed.

The so-called *Seborrhea* (*Dandruf*) is another common problem. It is seen as white flakes or specks on scalp and on hair. The cause is not known but the flakes are just the dead scalp tissue. In a young infant it may form a thick layer over the head, giving it the name *cradle cap*.

A Cetevalon or Savlon shampoo helps to get rid of seborrhea. If it does persist, see your doctor. If he agrees, use a cream, *Pragmatar*, as directed. I have found it very effective. Resistant cases may need a steroid cream for topical application. Do not forget to take care of the child's cleanliness and nutrition.

Pyoderma is a skin infection caused by the bacteria, *Streptococcus* or *staphylococcus*. The blisters or yellow-crusted sores appear on legs, hands and other parts of the body. Your doctor would generally prescribe gentian violet (or an antibiotic ointment if pyoderma is severe) for local application together with oral or injectable penicillin. The response is good to this treatment. But, do not forget that pyoderma is always a mirror of poor hygiene. So, take care of this aspect if you do not want your child to have future recurrences and to spread the disease to other members.

Eczema ia a sort of allergy to something which is often not easy to find out. Itching eruptions appear especially over cheeks, in the folds and over exposed areas of legs. It is likely to take long to disappear. So, have patience and cooperate with the treating doctor. The fact that it is not contagious is noteworthy.

Kidney ailments

If your child has fever, frequency of micturition, and painful micturition, he seems to be suffering from *urinary tract infection*. Urine examination, if the diagnosis is correct, will show numerous pus cells.

Following skin infection or tonsillitis, a child may develop puffiness of the eyes, fever and lethargy and pass scanty but bloody urine. He seems to be suffering from *acute nephritis.* Your doctor may find that the child has slight rise in his blood pressure and that the urine shows numerous red cells.

In *nephrotic syndrome,* the child develops swelling over feet and legs which steadily spreads to the rest of the body. Blood pressure is usually normal. Urine shows gross proteinuria.

Count on your doctor for diagnosis and management of any of these problems.

Diabetes mellitus

In certain individuals, a special type of gland (pancreas designed to produce a substance, "insulin", which plays an important role in making use of the carbohydrates (sugar starch) we eat, does not function well. As a result, the sugar is lost in urine and abnormal waste products accumulate in the body, causing many problems, the worst being unconsciousness (coma).

Childhood diabetes, also referred to as *growth-onset diabetes,* usually has an acute onset with excessive thirst, excessive frequency of micturition (more marked at night), excessive hunger, weight loss or failure to gain weight, weakness, tiredness and bodily pains. A child who was earlier dry may begin to suffer from bed-wetting. There may also occur inflammation and itching of the external genitals in girls (vulvitis), abdominal pain, nausea, vomiting, irritability and deterioration in school performance. At times the first manifestation forcing the parents to take the child to hopsital may be coma.

The doctors confirm the diagnosis by urine and blood examination.

Treatment is a highly specialised area and has to be in the form of insulin injections under medical care. The bigger child must, however, learn to test his own urine and to inject insulin himself. This stands him in good stead once he is back home after the initial hospital stay has achieved stabilisation.

Modern treatment does not stress on too much of dietary restriction. Concentrated carbohydrates like candies, sugar, sweets, chocolates and cakes should, however, be avoided.

Remember that hypoglycemic attacks (when glucose level in blood considerably falls below the desired) may cause naughtiness, behavioural change, fainting and even convulsions. At the earliest sign of such a problem, the child should eat a biscuit or two.

Growing pains

A proportion of the children complain of leg pains—usually involving muscles—towards the end of the day with, at times, recurrence during night for weeks on end. Flat feet and cramps in the calf muscles are thought to be the cause in a majority of them.

No doubt, growing pains have nothing to do with rheumatic fever in which the pains involve the joints specifically.

Nevertheless, a medical check-up is in order. Most doctors like to prescribe a pain-killer towards the evening as also calcium therapy for a number of weeks.

Hydrocele

Hydrocele is excessive accumulation of fluid around testicle so that the sac appears many times bigger than its normal size. This is a normal observation in newborns, the swelling receding as the baby grows.

At times, an older boy may have a chronic hydrocele. This needs an operation.

Hernias

Umbilical hernia is seen as a protruding swelling at the navel. It swells up on coughing or crying. In a large majority of the cases it regresses on its own by the age of 6 to 9 months or maximum 18 months. If it does not, the doctors go ahead for an operative correction.

The old practice of strapping the umbilical hernia with or without a large coin may actually interfere with its spontaneous closure and stands condemned.

Inguinal hernia is a recurrent swelling at the groin, at times involving the scrotum as well. This is due to a weak point in the abdominal wall so that intestines are allowed to protrude through it. It becomes apparent when the child coughs, cries, strains in some way or stands up, and slips back up into the abdomen when the child lies down quietly.

There is, however, a potential danger. Occasionally, the intestine may get struck in the passage, refusing to return to its original site. Consequent upon this, the blood vessels may get kinked and virtually shut off, leading to death of the intestinal tissue. The so-called "strangulation" or "obstruction" is manifested in the form of abdominal pain and vomiting. Never try to manually push the lump into the abdomen. You must remove the child immediately to the hospital. During the journey, elevate his hips on a pillow and cheer him up. This procedure may help in the reduction of the obstruction. If it fails, there is every chance the surgeon will go in for an emergency surgery.

For this reason, it is a policy to have the inguinal hernia operated as early as possible. Delaying the operation may mean an invitation to stragulation which can prove fatal if not attended to immediately.

Phimosis

In very many newborns, foreskin (prepuce) may be somewhat adherent to the underlying skin so that it cannot easily be retraced. In due course, it gets corrected without any special treatment.

Occasionally, however, the condition may persist, causing bulging of the foreskin on passing urine. This needs surgical correction which may, at times, amount to circumcision, i.e. chopping off the foreskin in toto. You may note that circumcision is a religious biding for Mohammedans and Jews.

Malnutrition

Mild to moderate nutritional deprivation involving primarily the calories and proteins over a prolonged period is met with by a child by slowing down his growth, the so-called *nutritional dwarfing* being the result. Such a child is relatively less active and more prone to infections.

Severe deprivation may take two forms. On one end of the scale is *nutritional marasmus* in which there is gross wasting of muscles and fat under the skin so that he is reduced to sheer skin and bones.

On the other end of the scale is what is termed *kwashiorkor* in which, though there is marked wasting of the muscles, the child looks bloated because of retention of water. He is listless, showing no interest in the surroundings. Hair is usually light-coloured, rough or silky and sparse, leaving bald areas over the scalp. Skin is often rough, dry and sore; at times there may be a patchy rash over vast areas, especially over feet and legs. Besides anaemia, there may be many other mineral and vitamin deficiencies, especially vitamin A deficiency (xerophthalmia) in which earliest manifestation is night blindness. In most children with kwashiorkor, an attack of diarrhoea, pneumonia, whooping cough or measles precedes the onset of full-blown disease.

Some children with gross protein-energy malnutrition may show a combination of picture of kwashiorkor and marasmus. The nomenclature, *marasmic-kwashiorkor*, may well be quite appropriate in them.

At times, an infant with a picture resembling kwashiorkor minus swelling over legs and feet may develop tremors which disappear or considerably regress during sleep. This condition is known as *infantile tremor syndrome*.

Xerophthalmia or vitamin A deficiency occurs in some 10 per cent of school-going children. It may occur as such or in association with protein-energy malnutrition, more so in kwashiorkor. Its earliest manifestation is that the eyes fail to adapt to dim light or dark, the so-called "night blindness". If the condition remains unattended, what results is dryness of conjuctiva (the white membrane) which becomes rough and muddy. All too soon, triangular raised foamy white patches appear over the white area. These are called "Bitot spots". Thereafter, the cornea (dark circular area in the centre) is involved and its varying stages of destruction may be seen. Destruction of cornea is called "keratomalacia" which is a sign of permanent blindness.

Rickets is a disease of growing children, resulting from deficiency of vitamin D. Manifestation include excessive sweating, particularly over the forehead even in cold weather, a somewhat big head with prominences at the forehead and sides, patency of fontanelle (the diamond-shaped area in the front portion of the head) beyond the age of 18 months, delayed dentition, bead-like swellings over the chest wall, widening of wrists and delayed walking. As the child begins to put weight on legs, there may result their deformity in the form of bow legs or knock knees.

B-complex deficiency usually manifests in the form of soreness of the lips, mouth or tongue.

Scurvy results from vitamin C deficiency and is only infrequently seen now in its full-blown form. Its manifestations include excessive irritability with tenderness of the legs, bloody spongy gums, bleeding from various sites and rough dry skin with minute bleeding spots at the hair roots.

Attention to proper nutrition of the infant and the child (including breast-feeding for as long as feasible and introduction of semi-solids and solids from the age of 3-4 months), his periodic check-ups for evaluating growth and any disease with proper treatment, and preventive vaccination go a long way in safeguarding against various types of malnutrition.

Cerebral palsy

You, at times, come across children with stiffness of the extremities, difficulty in holding objects, delayed or no walking, delayed or abnormal speech, or abnormal movements of the body, more so that of the extremities. Often, there is some degree of mental retardation. A proportion of them may suffer from seizures.

Most of them may be cases of cerebral palsy, the ailment that results because of brain damage during, before or soon after birth. A difficult delivery, severe jaundice and neo-natal infections are its leading causes. The disease is non-progressive, not curable and not fatal. Permanent handicap is, however, its cornerstone.

Physiotherapy can do a lot of good to these children. Your aim should be to make the child self-reliant. To bring out the best in the child, you may need a special teacher who has a good grasp of medical, social and psychological problems of the child. To create awareness about the needs of cerebral palsy-affected children, *The Spastic Society of India* was launched in 1972. By now its Centres are actively in operation in New Delhi, Bombay, Calcutta and Madras.

Mental retardation

Children with low learning capacity, poor maturation and inadequate social adjustment are grouped under this label. Their intelligence quotient (IQ) is under 85.

$$IQ = \frac{\text{Assessed mental age}}{\text{Chronological age}} \times 100$$

An IQ of 68 to 85 means borderline mental retardation, 52 to 67 mild mental retardation, 36 to 51 moderate mental retardation, 20 to 35 severe mental retardation and below 20 profound mental retardation.

Down's syndrome is a special variety of mental retardation in which the child has a peculiar face with upward slant of the eyes, widely-set eyes, depressed bridge of nose and protruding wrinkled tongue, retardation in physical growth, and typically sweet temperament. Also, called "monogolism", it is a chromosomal defect, usually occurring in babies of elderly women.

There is no effective treatment for Down's syndrome. Since there is a possibility of recurrence of the disease in the subsequent children, the parents must seek genetic counselling from the doctor or from the special centre he refers them to.

Cretinism or *congenital hypothyroidism* is another special type of mental retardation caused by congenital deficiency of a hormone, *thyroxine,* produced by the thyroid gland. Besides mental retardation, the child has delayed milestones, remarkable physical retardation, characteristics facies with rough features, widely-set eyes, depressed bridge of nose and large protruding tongue, low-set ears and short neck.

If recognised early, treatment with replacement therapy reverts the manifestations.

In the management of a child with mental retardation, the best course for the parents is to take the retarded child in their stride rather than curse their fate for the problem. The child must be accepted by them and rest of the family as he is. This helps in bringing out the best in him. Moreover, this gives him a good start in life.

Where should a mentally retarded child live: in an institution or at home? This is a rather ticklish question. Though many studies have now convincingly demonstrated that placement of the child in an institution has no edge over the home care, the parents can best decide on this in consultation with a family social agency or an agency designed to care the mentally retarded.

Convulsions

Convulsions are involuntary movements of one or more parts of the body and are quite frightening to the observers. These are caused by irritation of the brain cells by varying factors which differ from age to age. Though the commonest variety is what is termed *febrile convulsions,* in the age group 6 months to 3 years, as a result of rapidly rising temperature at the onset of tonsillitis, upper respiratory infection or pneumonia, every child with convulsions needs to be evaluated by the doctor. Only he can decide if the temporary treatment will suffice or the child requires to be put on a long-term medication.

In a typical case, the picture is characteristic. The child rolls up the eyes, clenches his teeth and makes rigid the body or parts of the body followed by convulsive shaking of the extremities and, at times, even the trunk. The breathing is heavy. Some frothing may appear at the mouth.

Sometimes, the child may pass urine or stools during the attack. The loss of consciousness may or may not occur. The attack is over within a few minutes in most cases after which the child usually sleeps.

What are you supposed to do when you suddenly are face to face with the child during convulsions? Rather than panicking for the medical aid, you should keep your cool. Make sure that the child doesn't hurt himself. Loosen his garments, particularly around the neck. If he appears to be biting the tongue, try to keep the jaws separated with a tooth brush handle or some such thing. After the attack, let the child be kept comfortably lying in a normal sleeping position. If you find that he is running a high fever, it will be very much in order to bring down the temperature by cold sponging, using lukewarm water.

In case a doctor becomes available and the child is still convulsing, he would give an injection of an anti-convulsant drug such as diazepam to control the attack. Afterwards, he would concentrate at finding the exact cause through detailed history-taking, clinical examination and, if needed, certain investigations. Do cooperate with him to provide the child the best possible treatment.

Let no mistake be made that, though in a large majority of the cases childhood convulsions are benign with no evidence of recurrence, these can be a manifestation of as serious a problem as meningitis or encephalitis (brain infection), septicemia (blood sepsis) or brain tumor. The term, *epilepsy*, is employed in situations in which the individual suffers from repeated convulsive attacks without any obvious cause. Long-term drug treatment aims at reducing the frequency and intensity of attacks.

Remember that sprinkling cold water over the child's face or making the child smell a shoe (a common practice in the folks) does no good to the child.

Meningitis

Meningitis is an inflammation of the membranes sheathing the brain and spinal cord. The original focus of infection may be elsewhere in the form of ear discharge, boil, pneumonia or tuberculosis. In newborns, the commonest focus is a septic umblicus. The causative organism may be bacteria (e.g. menigococcal meningitis cases have occurred in India, including Delhi and Agra, over recent years in epidemic proportions) virus, or, infrequently parasitic.

Manifestations of the serious disease include fever, headache, change in level of consciousness, vomiting, neck stiffness and convulsions. In newborn, manifestations may be as simple as refusal to feed, excessive crying or poor activity, jitteriness, twitching etc. Meningitis becomes a strong possibility if the umbilicus is unhealthy.

Such a child should be immediately shifted to the hospital where the doctors nearly always take action to establish the diagnosis by, among other investigations, lumbar puncture. The test consists in obtaining a small amount of fluid from the spinal canal through a needle inserted in the lower part of the spine by an expert. This fluid is then examined for information.

The child with meningitis is best treated in the hospital. Delay in instituting treatment or its poor compliance means not only complications but also a fair chance of losing the child.

Encephalitis

This, like meningitis, is a serious disease of the brain characterised primarily by inflammation of the brain cells. The medical symptoms are on the similar lines as in meningitis. Remember only the doctor can differentiate whether it is meningitis or encephalitis. That may need investigations like lumbar puncture.

Burns

Burns are a common accidental problem in children. These may be caused by chemicals, hot liquids, fire, crackers, or electricity.

Burns are classified as 10 per cent, 30 per cent or 50 per cent according to the magnitude of the body area involvement. They may be *first degree* (involving only superficial layer of skin and characterised by redness, little swelling and pain), *second degree* (relatively deeper involvement and characterised by spotted appearance, blister formation, swelling and pain), and *third degree* (deep tissue destruction with complete loss of all skin layers and absence of pain).

For first degree burns, immerse the affected area in cold water. Later cover loosely with a clean cloth or gauze and bandage, if necessary.

Second degree burns, if extensive, can be dangerous, leading to dehydration, shock and superadded infection. These should also be treated as the first degree burns. However, the child should be removed to the hospital as soon as possible. Meanwhile, make sure you do not disturb the blisters and give the child plenty of fluids to make up for losses from the burnt area.

In case of third degree burns, treat the burnt area as discussed earlier, give the child plenty of oral fluids and remove him to the hospital immediately.

Remember, doctors like to give tetanus toxoid injection as a prophylactic measure in most cases of burns.

APPENDIX A

A Befitting Name for Your Child

Here're some nice names which are yet to become the "beaten track." You may find a suitable name for your little one out of this list.

Ankur	Shibani	Sunandan	Honey
Gagan	Tulna	Aditi	Dimple
Deepshika	Mekhala	Chirag	Pammi
Bhavana	Anchal	Anshu	Reema
Charoo	Kokila	Deepali	Reva
Disha	Abhimanyu	Aneema	Ruchi
Chetan	Anjuman	Abhimanshu	Shamma
Divya	Rajak	Anubhav	Neeti
Akshay	Namrita	Shammi	Robin
Mrigya	Richa	Gomti	Monish
Kunal	Nishant	Abhinay	Rasik
Manav	Navneet	Varun	Raveesh
Komal	Savarkar	Tarun	Raval
Gitanshu	Veenu	Mridu	Ella
Karishma	Rahul	Anusuya	Ambar
Amrish	Vishal	Sukriti	Vilas
Ashutosh	Virju	Bhoomika	Vaman
Gaurav	Vaishali	Boski	Gulzareen
Ravinder	Ujjwal	Kavi	Sumeet
Shallu	Neeraj	Rishi	Nagraja
Supriya	Akash	Kavita	Tehmina
Deepti	Kaveesh	Shefali	Arti
Payal	Adil	Ketak	Piyush
Nancy	Upasana	Suraksha	Promila
Reetika	Parikrama	Lokpriya	Ruchika
Nikul	Anupama	Ankush	Gitika

Ridhi	Mandeep	Aditya	Feroza
Sarjoo	Aparna	Chitra	Freny
Deepika	Neera	Saurab	Mayur
Udhay	Rajat	Heemanshu	Mona
Ipshita	Novy	Surbi	Kanu
Megha	Abhinav	Arjun	Sujay
Anuj	Manu	Namita	Sumitra

APPENDIX B

Ten Basic Rights of the Child as Per the United Nation's Declaration of 1959

1. The child shall be brought up in a spirit of understanding, friendship, peace and universal brotherhood and shall not be exposed to racial, religious or other forms of discrimination.

2. The child shall be protected against all forms of neglect, cruelty exploitation and traffic and shall not be permitted to be employed till an appropriate minimum age.

3. The child shall, in all circumstances, be among the first to receive protection and relief.

4. The child is entitled to free and compulsory elementary education and such an education as is in his best interest for which the parents are to be responsible.

5. The child is entitled to grow up in an atmosphere of affection and moral and material security with public authorities taking care of children without families or other support.

6. The physically, mentally or socially handicapped child shall be entitled for special treatment, education and appropriate care.

7. The child shall have the right to adequate nutrition, housing, recreation and medical services, including special health care, and protection and parental and postnatal care for the mother.

8. The child shall be entitled to a name and a nationality.

9. The child shall enjoy special protection to be able to develop in every way in conditions of freedom and dignity.

10. All children—irrespective of their race, colour, sex or creed of their parents—shall be entitled to these rights.

APPENDIX C

Fifteen Principles of India's Current Policy for Children

1. A comprehensive health programme for all children.
2. Provision of nutrition services for children.
3. Provision of health care, nutrition and nutrition education for expectant and nursing mothers.
4. Free and compulsory education up to the age of 14, informal education for pre-schoolers, and efforts to reduce wastage and stagnation in school.
5. Out of school education for those not having access to formal education.
6. Promation of games, recreation and extracurricular activities in schools and community centres.
7. Special programmes for children from weaker sections.
8. Facilities for education, training and rehabilitation for children in distress.
9. Protection against neglect, cruelty and exploitation.
10. Banning of employment in hazardous occupations and in heavy work for children.
11. Special treatment, education, rehabilitation and care of physically handicapped, emotionally disturbed or mentally retarded children.
12. Priority for protection and relief of children in times of national distress and calamity.
13. Special programmes to encourage talented and grieved children particularly from the weaker sections.
14. That the paramount consideration in all relevant laws is "interests of children".
15. Strengthening family ties to enable children to grow within the family neighbourhood and community environment.

APPENDIX D

National Children's Fund

This Fund was established in 1979, the International Year of the Child, by the Government of India, in order to help the voluntary agencies implement programmes for the welfare and development of the children.

The Fund is administered by a Board that includes the Union Minister for Social Welfare as ex-officio Chairman and the Union Minister of State for Social Welfare as working Chairman. The Director, National Institute of Public Cooperation and Child Development, New Delhi, is the Secretary-cum-Treasurer of the Fund.

National Children's Fund seeks to offer financial assistance to voluntary agencies for implementing programmes for the welfare of the children, including rehabilitation of destitute children, those in the pre-school age group (0-5 years) in particular. Priority consideration is given to children belonging to Scheduled Castes and Scheduled Tribes. Stress is laid on innovative projects in the field of child welfare not otherwise covered by any agency of the Government.

All individuals and institutions are requested to donate to this Fund liberally. All contributions to the Fund are exempt from income tax under Section 80(G) of the Income Tax Act.

Donations may be deposited in any branch of the State Bank of India for credit to the account of the Fund No. 3200 in the Rail Bhavan (New Delhi) Branch of the Bank, or sent to the

Secretary Treasurer,
National Children's Fund,
National Institute of Public Cooperation
& Child Development,
Siri Institutional Area,
Opp. Hauz Khas Police Station,
New Delhi-110016

Voluntary organisations seeking financial assistance from the Fund may get in touch with the Secretary-Treasurer at the above address. The assistance, as a rule, is limited to 90 per cent of the estimated cost of the project, provided that, the quantum of assistance does not exceed one lakh rupees.